SHOP DESIGN SERIES

CAFE & RESTAURANT

50 Outstanding Dinner, Beer and Cafe Restaurants

目次

CONTENTS

Abbreviations 略号

A／C——Air Conditioner 空調機
BC——Beer Cooler ビールクーラー
Bottle Cooler ボトルクーラー
CR——Cloakroom クロークルーム
CTR——Counter カウンター
DCT——Dish up Counter ディシャップカウンター
DF——Drinking Fountain ドリンクディスペンサー
DS——Duct Space ダクトスペース
DSP——Display Space ディスプレイスペース
DT——Display Table ディスプレイテーブル
DW——Dumb waiter, Lift ダムウエーター・リフト
EH——Entrance Hall エントランスホール
ELEC——Electrical Room 電気室
ESC——Escalator エスカレーター
ELV——Elevator, Lift エレベーター
F——Freezer 冷凍庫
FR——Fitting Room フィッティングルーム
FRF——Freezer & Refrigerator 冷凍冷蔵庫
GL——Ground Level 基準地盤面
Hg——Hanger ハンガー
IM——Ice Maker 製氷器
LF——Lighting Fixture 照明器具
LR——Locker Room ロッカールーム
MIR——Mirror 鏡
MECH——Mechanical Room 機械室
MWC——Men's Water Closet 男子用便所
PA——Public Address 音響機器
PN——Pantry パントリー
PS——Pipe Shaft パイプシャフト
PT——Package Table 包装台
R——Register, Cashier レジスター
REFR——Refrigerator 冷蔵庫
SC——Show Case ショーケース
Sh——Shelf 棚
SP——Speaker スピーカー
SPC——Sample Case サンプルケース
SR——Staff Room 従業員室
SS——Service Station サービスステーション
Service Area サービスエリア
ST——Stage 陳列（台）ステージ
SW——Show Window ショーウインドー
T——Table テーブル
VM——Vending Machine 自動販売機
WA——Waiting Area 待合スペース
WBR——Windbreak Room 風除室
WT——Work Table 調理台・作業台
WWC——Women's Water Closet 女子用便所
WH——Warehouse 倉庫・ストックルーム

CL——Clear Lacquer クリアラッカー
CB——Concrete Block コンクリートブロック
EL——Enamel Lacquer エナメルラッカー
EP——Emulsion Paint エマルジョンペイント
FB——Flat Bar フラットバー
FIX——Fixed Fitting はめ殺し
FL——Fluorescent Lamp 蛍光灯
HL——Hair-line Finish ヘアライン仕上げ
LGS——Light Gauge Steel 軽量鉄骨
OP——Oil Paint オイルペイント
OS——Oil Stain オイルステイン
PB——Gypsum Board, Plaster Board 石こうボード
PL——Plate 平板・プレート
RC——Reinforced Concrete 鉄筋コンクリート
S——Steel Frame 鉄骨
SRC——Steel Framed Reinforced Concrete
鉄骨鉄筋コンクリート
VP——Vinyl Paint ビニルペイント
@——Pitch ピッチ

本書は1990年から1993年までの月刊商店建築誌（増刊号を含む）に掲載された作品をセレクトし，構成したものです。作品に関するコメントは，編集者が雑誌に掲載された設計者とクライアントのコメントをもとに短い文章にまとめています。また，巻末の作品データ欄は雑誌掲載時のものですので，営業内容など変更になっている場合があります。

This book collects projects selected from Monthly Shotenkenchiku back numbers(including extra issues) published from 1990 through 1993, adding several new ones. All the texts except some of the new projects are summaries by the editor of comments by the designers and clients.

DINNER RESTAURANTS & THEME RESTAURANTS

1

緑と水に囲まれたアトリウムレストラン

ザ・ガーデン

東京都港区海岸1丁目11-1 ニューピア竹芝レストランコート3階

企画／東京ガス多角化推進部 ジェトファ・ザンク・オペレーターズ
設計／ジェトファ・ザンク・オペレーターズ 遠藤 明 小松正美 鎌形幸男
協力／アートディレクション セッサ 植栽計画 ランドスケープハウス
施工／竹芝埠頭再開発第一期工事建築J.V.
ジェトファ・ザンク・オペレーターズ

Health Conscious Restaurant
THE GARDEN

Kaigan Minato-ku Tokyo, Designer JTFA & ZINK Operators Inc.

1. 道路側に面したゲートより客席F方向を見る
View from the gate to the Dining F
2. コロッシアムとよばれる中央客席Eの噴水
The fountain of the dining E

2

4

●ハイテクに支えられた巨大な空中庭園

大昔，バビロンには世界の七不思議の一つといわれた空中庭園があった。東京・竹芝桟橋のビル内部にできたこのレストランは，まさに現代の巨大な空中庭園である。

二つのビルを結ぶ地上３階のレベルに設けられた広さ約1900m²のアトリウムがすべてレストランとなっており，自然光がトップライトから降りそそぐ内部空間に緑があふれ，小川が流れる。九つのエリアに分けられた客席で，来客は“キュイジーヌ・ピュール”とネーミングされた低公害，低農薬野菜，放牧で育った牛，鶏，天然の魚介類を使用した安全性の高い料理を，人工的な自然の中で楽しむことができる。

このような環境を作り出すために，植物が必要としている地盤には重さが通常の1/6，深さが1/3ですむ超軽量人工土壌が導入され，また人工照明と空調を精密にコンピューターで制御して人間と植物が両立できるよう工夫されている。まさにこのレストランはハイテクによって再現された巨大な人工自然環境なのである。

3. 海側の客席Hより見たアトリウム全景
View of the atrium from the dining H
4. ベンジャミンの林に囲まれた客席Dの内部
View of the dining D
5. 人工地盤上に設けられた外観を道路側より見る
View of the facade from the street side

THE GARDEN

The Hanging Gardens of Babylon is one of the Seven Wonders of the ancient world. This restaurant opened in a building of Takeshiba pier might be described as a contemporary version of the hanging gardens.

Occupying fully a three floor level high atrium (1,900 square meter) between two buildings, the interior is filled with sunshine from top light and watercourses. There are nine dining areas for “cuisine pure” , which means non-polluted natural food (vegetables, beef, chicken, sea food, etc.) produced by the least artificial way with the least chemical nutrition in a natural environment. Special artificial soil was introduced to keep this garden and it weighted one ninth of the standard soil and it needed one third depth of standard material to maintain. Lighting and air-conditioning are meticulously controlled by computers to keep an optimum natural ambient. This project represents itself as a big man-made garden supported by high technology.

5

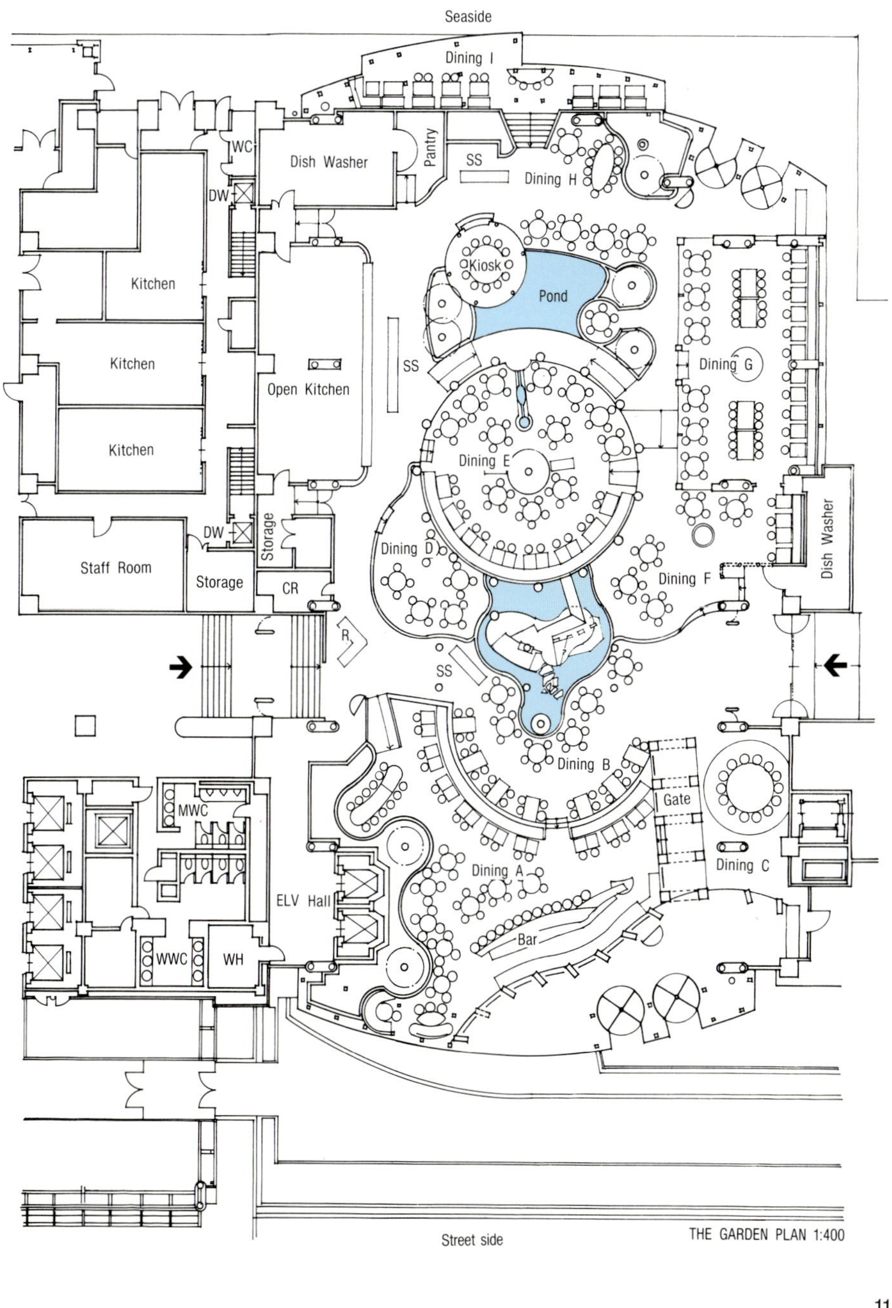

THE GARDEN PLAN 1:400

1

菓子工場跡地を再開発した大型複合レストラン

東京バモラ

東京都渋谷区笹塚1丁目50-1　笹塚NAビル

Restaurant TOKIO VAMOS-LA!!

Sasazuka Shibuya-ku Tokyo, Designer Kume Sekkei+TE.T.O.RA

設計／建築　久米設計　内装　テトラ　冨永俊三
施工／大成建設

1. 噴水より公開空地である中庭を通して見た北側外観
North view from the fountain
2. 吹き抜けに面した2階ブリッジよりバーコーナーを見る
View of the bar corner from the bridge

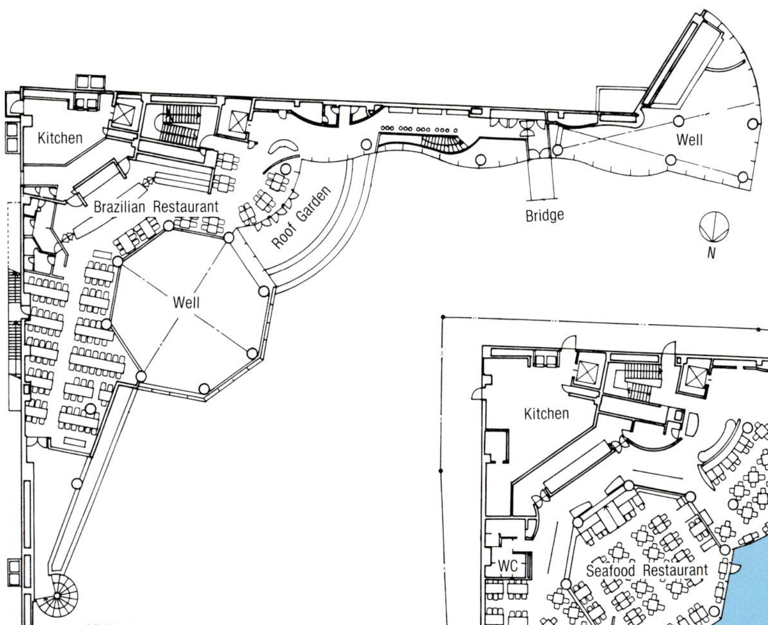

2F PLAN

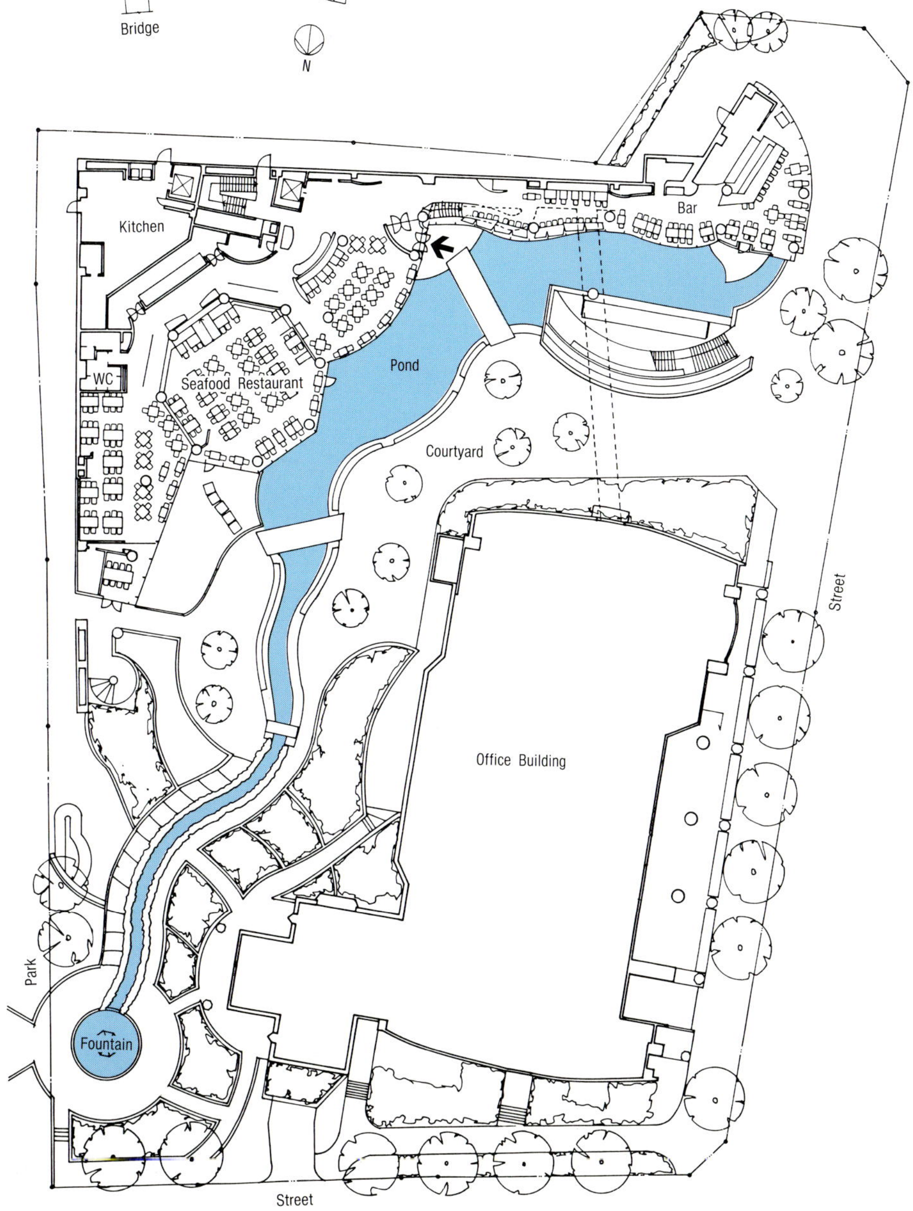

TOKIO VAMOS-LA!! 1F PLAN 1:600

● “食の新大陸発見” がコンセプト

都市化が進むなかで，周辺にある工場が郊外へ移転した後の跡地を，どう再開発するかは大きな問題である。東京・笹塚にできたこの大型複合レストランは，パンと菓子を製造販売している大手メーカーの，新たな道路計画により二つに分断されてしまった工場の一方の跡地を利用して企画された。

約5500㎡の広大な敷地には，レストランの他にオフィスビルが建てられたが，両者を隔てるものとして緑豊かな庭園が設けられ，中央を人工の川が流れている。レストランのコンセプトは大航海時代とされ，食の新大陸発見のため帆船で乗り出すという設定である。３階まで吹き抜けたガラス張りのメーンアトリウムには，このコンセプトに従って帆柱をイメージした銅板腐食仕上げの柱が林立し，帆を思わせるバナーが吊り下げられている。

内部は，１階が海鮮レストランとフードバー，２階がブラジルのシェラスコレストランで合計500席以上の客席を持ち，また，地下１階が会員制のスポーツクラブ，３階がオーナー会社の所蔵する美術品を展示するギャラリーとなっている。

3

3. シーフードレストランの中央アトリウム
The atrium of the seafood restaurant

TOKIO VAMOS-LA.!!

Urbanization moves factories from the metropolitan area to suburbs and leaves a number of empty lots, which will be targets of re-developing plan.

Built on a ex-factory site of a big bread and confectionery factory, this restaurant complex was born. The site was divided by an highway plan. Within a 5,500 square meters site, there are the restaurants and an office building, and both are separated by a garden with rich plants and a watercourse.

The concept of the restaurant is "the era of sailing ship adventure", and visitors are member of a sailing ship for the new continent for dining. The main glazed atrium of three floor level has a forest of masts with rusted copper plates. Long curtain drapes suggest banners or sails.

The first floor is a seafood restaurant and a food bar, the second floor a Brazilian churrasco restaurant with seats for 100 people, the third floor a gallery of the company owner's fine art collection, and the basement a sports club.

1

大阪ウオーターフロントのカフェ+レストラン

アミエル&フリスコ

大阪府大阪市住之江区南港北1丁目6

設計／榎本文夫アトリエ
施工／イシマル　田畑光啓
アオキ工芸　青木 満

Cafe AMIELLE & Restaurant FRISCO

Nanko-kita Suminoe-ku Osaka, Designer Fumio Enomoto

1. 入り口より待合を通して1階カフェ客席方向を見る
1F: View of the cafe from the entry
2. 吹き抜けに面した1階カフェの大テーブル席
1F: Big table seatings of the cafe

2

3

4

●自然環境と人工環境との対比
大阪・南港地区は大阪湾に面したウオーターフロントであり，アジア太平洋トレードセンター（ATC）など大規模な施設が次々と建設されている巨大な開発地域である。この地区に本社を新築したファッションメーカーの別棟にカフェ・アミエル＆レストラン・フリスコはある。
１階のカフェと地下１階のレストランを大きな吹き抜けで結んだ２層の空間は，地域にふさわしく，海に面した自然環境と巨大なビルによる人工環境の混在デザインをそのコンセプトとしている。吹き抜けの下部にある地下１階の床は御影石の乱貼りで，大きくとられた目地には人工芝が敷かれており，本物の自然とフェイクな人工材との対比が試みられている。また，フロストガラスで仕切られた地下１階奥部分には人工植物による庭園が設けられ，逆にテーブル上には生け花がおけるように花ビンを組み込んでいるのも，人工と自然の対比というデザインの意図を表現するための手法である。

3. 地下1階レストランを1階カフェより見る
View of the restaurant from the cafe
4. 地下1階レストランの入り口アプローチ
B1F: Approach of the restaurant

AMIELLE & FRISCO
Nanko, a vast developing water-front area of Osaka with a number of ongoing big projects, such as A.T.C. (Asian & Pacific Trade Center), etc. A cafe Amielle and a restaurant Frisco opened in an annex building of a fashion manufacturer.
Connecting the first floor (for cafe) and the basement (restaurant), the two-floor level space matches to the environment, expressing a concept of the mixed ambient of the nature (the sea) and the artificial (skyscrapers).
The basement floor is covered with granite mosaic with fake turf in gaps to contrast the texture of natural and artificial materials. Divided by frosted glass walls, an area of the basement has a garden-like space with artificial plants. Real plants are arranged in a vases on tables as accents of the space.

5

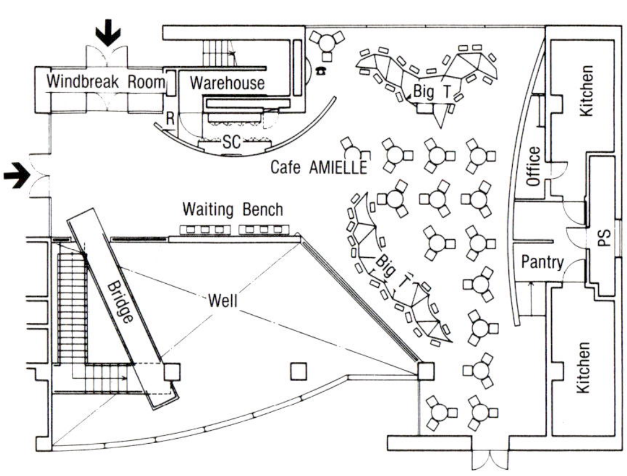

AMIELLE & FRISCO 1F PLAN 1:400

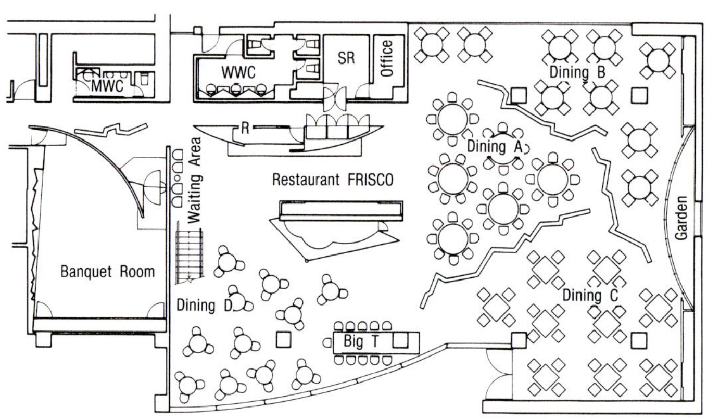

B1F PLAN

5. 地下1階レストランの大テーブル席より客席C方向を見る
B1F: View of the dining C from the big table

1万本の真竹乱れ編みスクリーンに包まれたレストラン

サトー

東京都港区赤坂3丁目8-1　赤坂アルトビル6階

設計／プラスチックスタジオアソシエイツ　高山不二夫
施工／メッセ　和田 清　高橋 敦

Restaurant SATO

Akasaka Minato-ku Tokyo, Designer Fujio Takayama

1. 厨房への通路から客席A方向を見る
View of the dining A from the kitchen entry

1

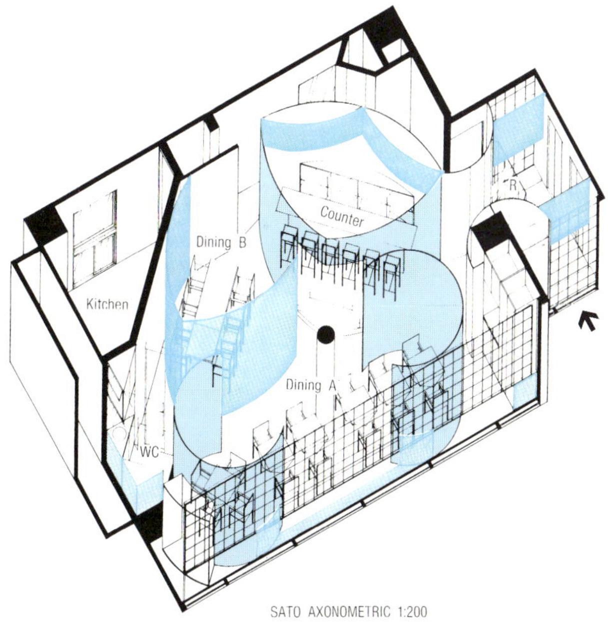

SATO AXONOMETRIC 1:200

●竹の美しさと生命感を表現
竹は日本だけでなくアジア全域に見られ，東洋を代表する植物といえる。昔から容器や生活用具に加工利用されてきたが，このレストランの場合は，インテリアの主要なエレメントとしてスクリーンに使用された。
竹は地中では複雑に入り組んだ根を張っているが，地上では垂直に上へ上へと伸びる性質を持っている。このまっすぐに伸びる竹の美しさ，生命感，そうした竹本来の姿をデザインするのが設計の意図であった。あえてスクリーンの上下にフレームを取り付けていないのも，床から生え，天井を突き抜けて上へ伸びていくイメージを表現するためである。
約１万本の割り竹は一本一本，職人が手で編み上げたもので，その圧倒的な存在感とともに，近寄るごとに竹の持つしなやかさ，自然の素材感が伝わってくる。竹の隙間を通して伝わる光，空気，そして気配が不思議な調和を空間に生み出し，来客を包み込む。

2. 竹のスクリーンに囲まれた店内を入り口より見る
Whole view of the interior from the entry

SATO
Bamboos are not only common Japanese plants but also typical Asian plants seen through almost all Asian countries.
From old times, bamboos were used to made into a vessels and other everyday goods. In this restaurant, the plants were used as screens and important design elements.
Bamboos have intricate roots under the ground and the trunk grow vertically upward. A designer of this project was attracted the beautiful straight line of trunks and strong vitality and he planed to express it. The bamboo screens have no frames above and under, the designer tried to express a image of bamboos growing from the floor penetrating the ceiling.
To make the screens, craft men wove about 10,000 pieces of bamboos, whose impression no visitors can ignore. Its flexibility, texture, atmosphere, the effect of light through screens. An aura of bamboo fills the air and surrounds people.

1

食と文化が融合した高級ディナーレストラン

東京ディナー

東京都港区西麻布４丁目11-42

Restaurant TOKYO DINNER

Nishi-azabu Minato-ku Tokyo, Designer Takeo Kumai

設計／アルコポリス　協力／構造設計　小林構造設計室　野崎設計事務所
施工／鹿島建設

1. 道路に面した入り口まわり夜景　**Night view of the entry from the street**
2. 道路と内部を遮断するファサードの大壁　**View of the facade from the street**

2

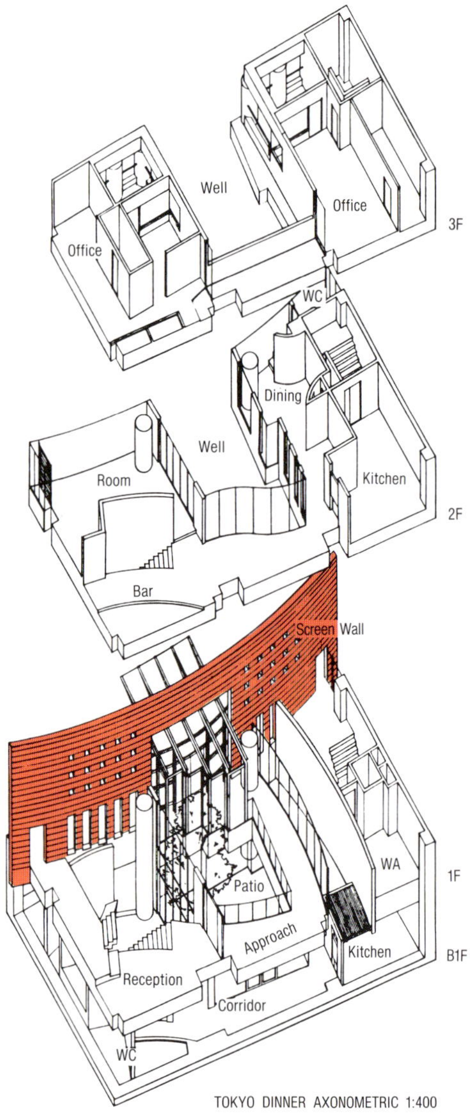

TOKYO DINNER AXONOMETRIC 1:400

3. 吹き抜けに面した2階個室内部　**2F: Interior view of the room**
4. 店内中央のパティオを1階アプローチ道路より見る　**1F: View of the patio from the approach**

3

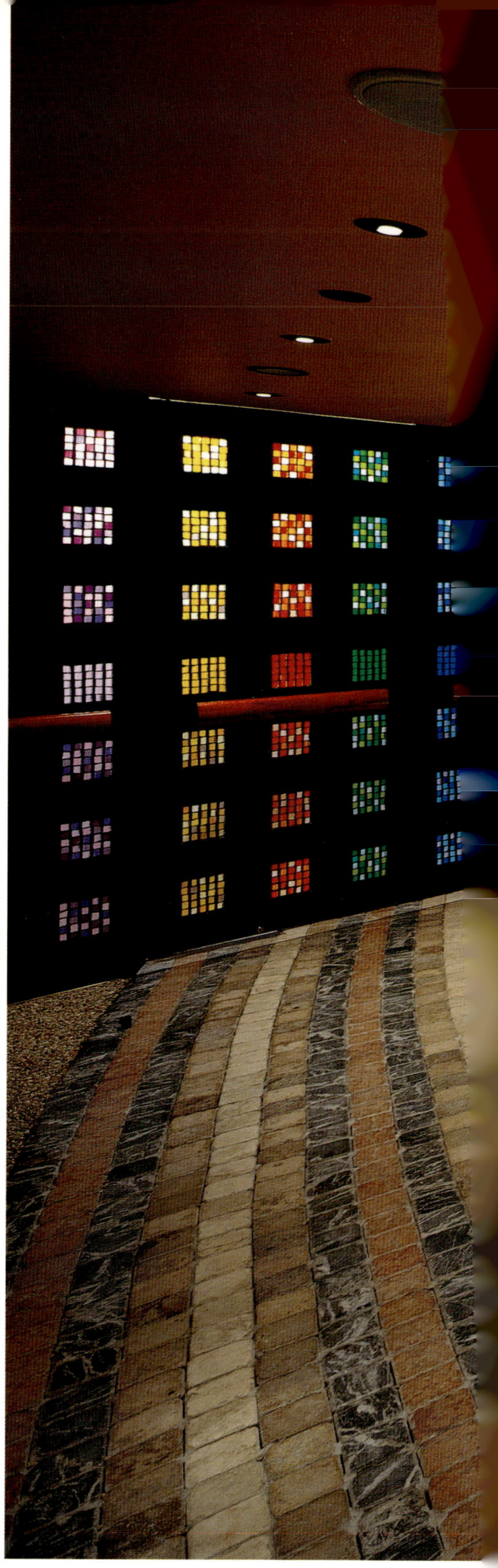

●湾曲した一枚の外部を隔絶する大壁

“食は文化なり”という言葉がある。食べることは，単に生理的な欲求をみたすだけでなく，食材や調理方法，マナーまでを含んだ多様な世界であるからだろう。東京には珍しく緑が豊富で，各国の大使館が点在する広尾にできたこのレストランは，食と文化を融合させ，おいしい料理と心からのもてなしとサービス，やすらぎのある建築の三つを合体させることを目的として企画された。

デザイン上の特徴は，通り抜けのクルマが多い道路か

4

ら内部空間を断絶するために高さ７メートル，幅20メートルの湾曲した１枚の大壁を屹立させていることである。大壁に穿たれた入り口をはいったスペースには，地下１階から３階まで吹き抜けたガラス張りのパティオが設けられ，中央に大きな木が植えられている。このパティオは内部空間の中心的な存在で，立体的な中庭として各階を有機的に連続させ，日本庭園の伝統的な手法としてヨーロッパの庭園にはない回遊性を建築にもたらしている。

TOKYO DINNER

A way of eating represents a culture. That means eating is not what we eat just to satisfy our appetite, for we choose food and cocking way by our own way and taste.

This restaurant in Hiroo, Tokyo which is a area with a number of foreign embassies, regards food and cocking as an aspect of culture, fusing nice dish, warm-hearted service, and comfortable interior.

To separate the restaurant from a busy street, a huge carved wall (h.7m, w.20m) stands on the front. Entering from the door of the wall, you reach a glazed patio from the basement to the third floor with a tall tree in the center. The patio is the core of this restaurant, functionally connecting each floor. It is quite a traditional Japanese style small court, slightly different from European style in its flexibility.

トップライトを持つホテル最上階のレストラン

ボーセジュール&エトワール

埼玉県川越市新富町1丁目22 川越プリンスホテル9階

Restaurant BEAUX SEJOURS & Bar Lounge ETOILE

Shintomi-cho Kawagoe-shi Saitama
Designer Seibu Construction Co.,Ltd.

設計／西武建設
施工／建築　西武建設
　　　内装　綜合デザイン

●陽だまりとパサージュのダブルイメージ
東京から電車で約1時間の場所にある川越市は，小江戸とよばれた古い城下町である。新築された駅ビルの一部としてオープンしたホテルの最上階である9階に，このレストラン&バーは位置する。ホテルを代表する施設として，ホテルの基本的テーマ"山・風・雲"をシンボリックに表現することが意図された。
最上階であることを利用して設けられた巨大なガラス張りの天窓は，縁側という陽だまりの中で育まれた居心地の良い，軽やかな温か味のある感覚を再現したものであり，同時にパリのパサージュをイメージしたものである。高い天窓には光をコントロールするためにグラスファイバー製のスクリーンが導入され，入ってくる自然光を拡散し，柔らかく増幅する。またスクリーンには箔押しされた金によって天女の羽衣のように微妙な色彩と淡く軽やかな空気の流れを空間にもたらしている。天井から吊り下げられた照明器具は，この町の最大の祭りに使われるちょうちんを現代風にアレンジしたものである。

1. 個室A側より見たレストラン全景。天井のグラスファイバー製スクリーンは開閉できる
View of the restaurant from the room A

BEAX SEJOURS & ETOILE
Accessible by about one hour train trip from Tokyo, Kawagoe, an old castle city in Saitama prefecture is called one of "small Edo-like cities".
This bar & restaurant opened on the ninth floor of a hotel in a new station building and it expresses hotel's design concept of "Mountains, Winds, and Clouds" with symbolic elements.
As it locates on the top of the hotel, it has huge skylight to let sunshine in to relax customers. Also the design of skylight depends on a image of passage in Paris.
Glass fiber screens were installed to control or modify the sun light. The screen, with the golden pattern and the color of the heavenly robe of angels, seems to create ethereal air in the interior. Hanging lamps represent Japanese lanterns which are used in a big festival in this city.

1

2. バー・エトワールの内部を入り口側から見る **View of the bar from the entry side**

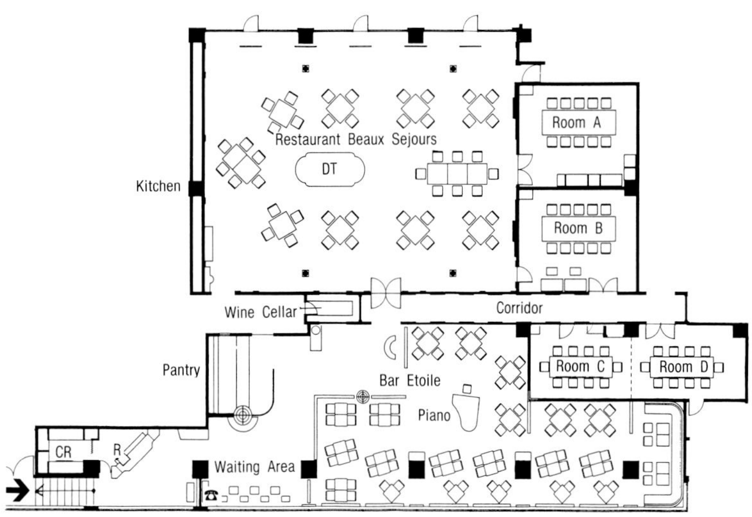

BEAUX SEJOURS & ETOILE PLAN 1:400

外部の自然と一体化したフレンチレストラン

ベルダンテュール

愛媛県松山市歩行町１丁目13-7

French Restaurant BELL DENTURE

Kachi-machi Matsuyama-shi Ehime
Designer Kazuhiro Sagawa

設計／ライフ・スペース　佐川和弘　森野和幸
協力／構造　樋口構造設計　樋口清二
設備　設備企画"N"　中矢大三　山本浩二
施工／新東建設

1. 道路側より見た正面外観全景
View of the facade from the street

1

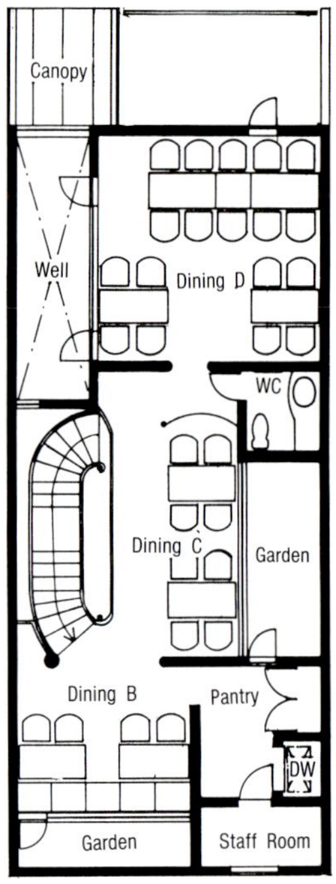

2F PLAN

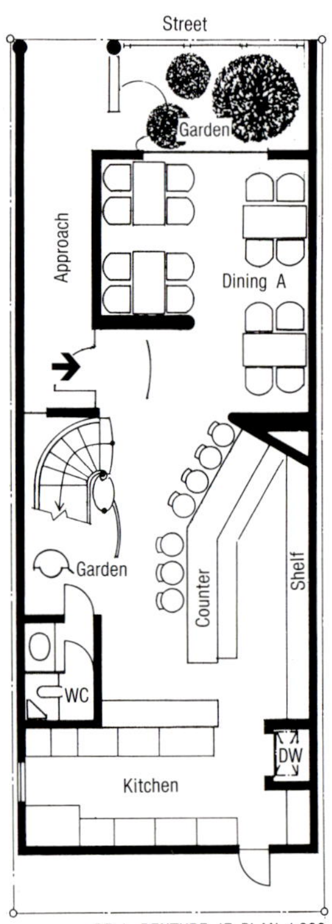

BELL DENTURE 1F PLAN 1:200

2

●"五感においしい時間"の提供
四国・松山市は瀬戸内海に面した，温暖な気候に恵まれた地方都市である。市の中心から歩いて５分余りの閑静な住宅街の一角にできたこのレストランは，周囲の豊かな自然環境を店内に取り込み，食事をするにふさわしい五感を満足させる空間を目指してデザインされた。
そのために，１階の客席と外部道路の間に庭が設けられているだけでなく，２階の客席にも２カ所に庭が作られ，雨や風，太陽などの自然が感じられるようになっている。また，さりげなく光を注ぎ込むトップライトは空を表し，移動式カーテンは雲，鉄パイプは森，その先端のアッパーライトはきらめく星，ジュータンは川の流れ，階段は滝，アプローチの敷き石はさざ波を表現したものである。
時流を追うのではなく，自然を媒体とした豊かな空間と時間を感じさせる店づくりは，地方都市におけるゆとりと落ち着きを感じさせるデザインとなっている。

2. 天窓のある2階客席Cより客席B方向を見る
2F: View of the dining C and staircase

BELL DENTURE

Commanding a splendid view of the Seto Inland Sea and favored with the mild climate, Matsuyama is a rural city in Shikoku island of Japan. Five minutes walk from the center of the city takes you to this restaurant in a quiet residential area.

It was designed to utilize the surrounding beautiful natural environment for customers to dine in a joyful atmosphere appealing to their sense of beauty.

A tiny garden was made between the interior and exterior and the same gardens were located on the second floor behind two dining areas with glass wall in the back. Customers can see and feel rain, wind, sunshine, and other natural things. Skylight, like the sky, let the sun light in and movable curtains also represent the sky. Iron pipes are forest and lamps on them are shining stars. Rugs express a rivers, stairs are cascades and pavement of hallway are waves. Depending a theme of the nature the interior looks does not look trendy but calm and composed, becoming to this old rural city.

1

リラクセーションクラブと合体したディナーレストラン

天王洲倶楽部

東京都品川区東品川２丁目２-８　スフィアタワー天王洲24〜27階

Restaurant TENNOZ CLUB

Higashi-Shinagawa Shinagawa-ku Tokyo
Designer Akira Ojima

企画／スフィアコーポレーション
基本設計　キャビネ　オジマ　尾嶋 彰　実施設計　アークショップ　中村 薫
協力／大智設計　萩原達男　照明計画　ミンツデザイン　玉井俊二
施工／乃村工芸社

1. 受付わきに配された27階中央のホール　**27F: View of the hall from the reception**
2. 吹き抜けに面した27階 和食エリアより26階を見る　**27F: View of the staircase from the Japanese restaurant**

2

3

●フランス19世紀前半の様式を忠実に再現
西洋建築を取り入れる場合，日本では様式としてのかたちを模倣するだけに終わり，背後に潜む精神までも理解することは少なかった。新しく発展しつつある東京ウオーターフロントのオフィスビル最上部を占めるこのレストランは，高級なスポーツクラブの一部として誕生したものであり，古典フランス文化と日本文化の結合をコンセプトとしている。
コンセプトを実現するために取られた手法は，デザインのテーマとなったフランス19世紀前半の様式を，本物の技術と素材を使って忠実に追求することであった。建築的"伝統精神"を把握しながら，伝承された技法によって再現されたものは単なる模倣とは違い，デフォルメによる迎合も妥協も存在しないという考えかたによるものである。
石膏の成型，装飾金具，主な照明器具はルーブル美術館に品物を納めたという300年の伝統を持つフランスの金物工場にオーダーされ，また，工事の最終にはフランスから13人の職人が来日してペインティングの仕上げを行うなど，本物の再現に最大の努力が払われた。

3. 吹き抜けに面した27階のバーコーナー
27F: View of the bar corner
4. 窓側に面した26階のイタリアンレストラン客席
26F: View of the Italian restaurant

TENNOZ CLUB
It seemed that Japanese architecture superficially adopted Western style as a variation of styles without considering deeply the spirit behind it. This restaurant occupies the top of a office building of newly developing Tokyo water front area proclaims a concept of unification of French classical style and traditional Japanese style.
To achieve this tough concept, the 19th century French style as the main theme, was reproduced faithfully with real material and techniques. The result is that grasping traditional spirit of the architectural style with the use of traditional technology is far from imitation, with no compromise nor reconciliation by deformation.
The designer ordered plaster moldings, metal decorations, and main lamps for a 300 years old hardware factory purveyor to the Louvre. At the final stage of construction, 13 French craftsmen came to Japan to finish paintings. This one instance is enough to show the high quality of this project.

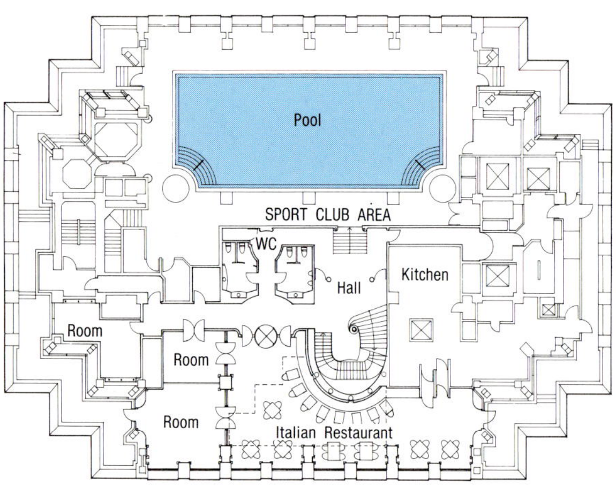

TENNOZ CLUB 26F PLAN 1:600

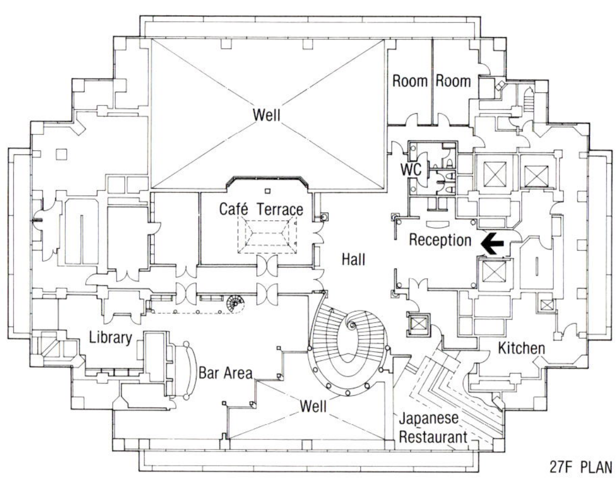

27F PLAN

4

ナチュラル・イメージを白木で表現したストラン

テラス モルチェ

東京都渋谷区広尾５丁目６－６ 広尾プラザ１階

Terrace MORTIER

Hiroo Shibuya-ku Tokyo, Designer Minoru Takeyama Architect & U／A

設計／竹山実建築綜合研究所　神山健一　高月純子
協力／テーブルウエアコーディネート　エデュース　木村ふみ　熊代登志子
施工／綜合デザイン　沢田正美

1. 入り口側から波形のパーティションに囲まれた客席Aを見る
View of the dining A from the cashier side

1

2

●オープンエアな雰囲気の表現
東京・広尾は高級住宅街であるとともに，各国大使館が点在し，ハイクラスの外国人が住む街として知られている。地下鉄・広尾駅そばにある広尾プラザは，ハイグレードな地域住民を対象にしたショッピングビルであり，中央のアトリウムに面してこのレストランはある。
カジュアルでアメリカ的な明るいイメージにしたいというクライアントの要望により，昼光の差し込むアトリウムに全面ガラスのサッシで面しているという条件を生かし，オープンエアのテラス的デザインが提案された。
床の素材を始め，ベジタブルバーなどの什器・家具類はすべて白木で統一されることにより，明るい大地の温もりを感じさせ，また，壁と天井は白色でフェードアウトさせることによって澄んだ空気を表現している。これらの素材感と色彩の統一からくる単調さを排除し，広がりのある空間を創り出すために微妙な凹凸やミラーを各所にちりばめるなどの配慮がデザイン上でさりげなくなされている。

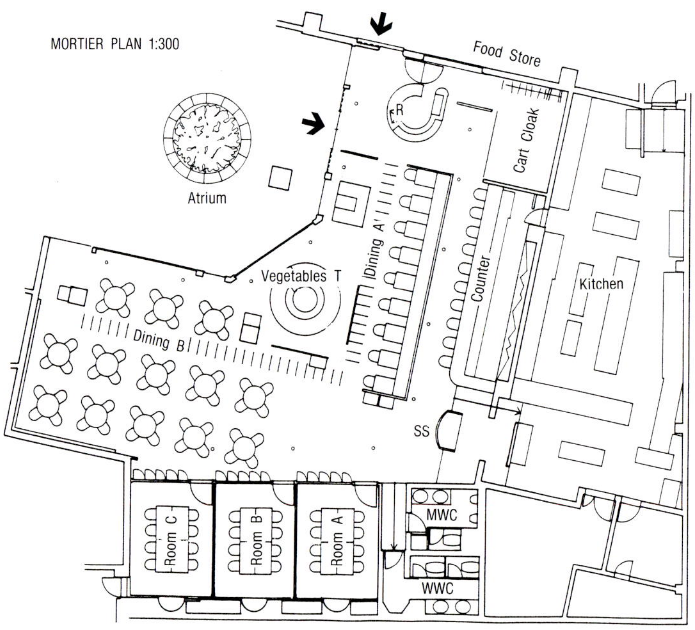

2. 明るくカジュアルな雰囲気の客席B
View of the dining B from the passage
3. 仕切りを取り払った個室Aより個室B方向を見る
Whole view of the room from the entry

MORTIER
Hiroo, Tokyo is a famous high class residential area with several foreign embassies and many foreigners living there. Hiroo Plaza near the subway station is a shopping complex for upper class residents in neighborhood. This restaurant is in there, facing the central atrium.
The client required an American casual, open atmosphere. Using the location facing the all glazed atrium, the restaurant was designed as open-air-like terrace style. Floor material, salad bar station, furniture were all made of unvarnished wood to create warmth of the earth. Walls and the ceiling are white for customers to imagine clean air. To keep the interior from being monotonous and subdue simplicity, subtle unevenness and mirrors were deliberately adopted.

3

1

アメリカンコミックから飛び出したレストラン

サーフ&ターフ

愛媛県松山市宮田町131-2　郵政弘済会ビル1階

Restaurant Bar SURF 'N TURF

Miyata-cho Matsuyama-shi Ehime
Designer Jordan Mozer

設計／ジョーダン・モザー
協力／アド　岩本嘉視　施工／アド

1. ウェーティングバーの擬人化されたスツール
   View of the waiting bar from the entry side
2. FRPのサボテンに囲まれた客席Aをトイレ側より見る
   View of the dining A from the lavatory side

2

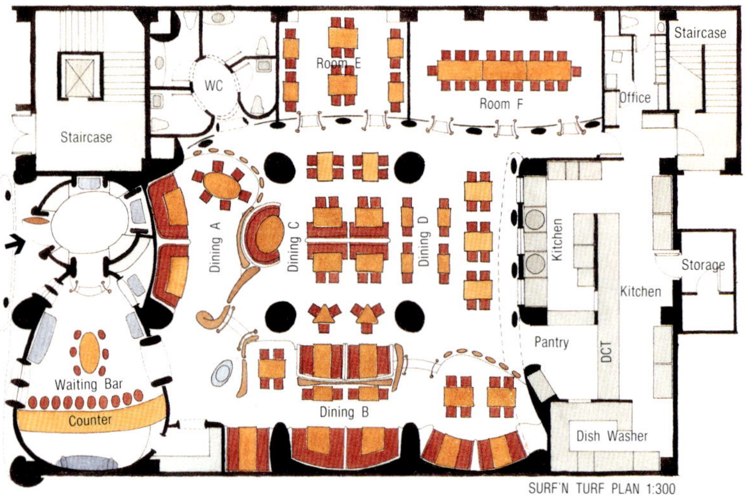

SURF'N TURF PLAN 1:300

3. 奥の個室E入り口まわりを客席Cより見る
View of the room E from the dining C
4. 厨房側より見た中央客席全景。コミックの世界をユーモラスに表現
Whole view of the dining hall from the kitchen side

3

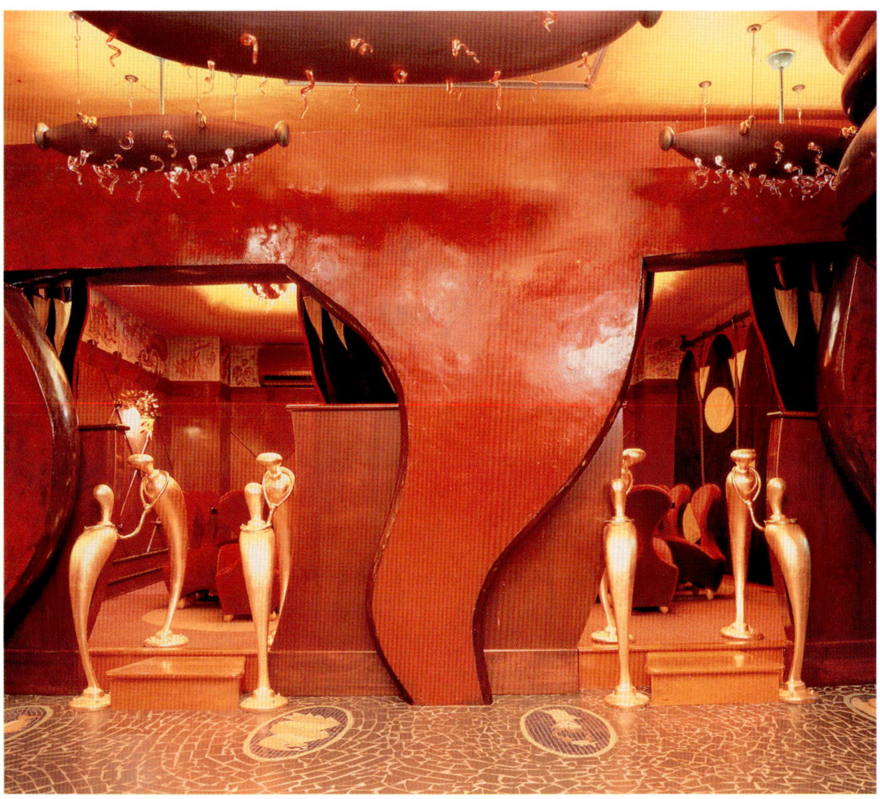

●ポップなユーモアを表現する

1960年代にアメリカとイギリスを中心として起こったポップ・アートは，雑誌やテレビなどの情報化社会におけるマスメディアのイメージやキャラクターを題材にし，別の価値を生み出そうとした。このムーブメントはアートだけでなく，デザインを含む広範な分野に影響を与え，ポップ・カルチャーを形成してきた。

四国の松山市にできたこのレストランは，アメリカのコミック漫画をテーマにしたもので，設計もアメリカ人ジョーダン・モザーの手になる。ショップを形成するデザインエ

4

レメントの多くは，遊び心に溢れ，愉快なデザインとなっている。たとえば，ドアハンドルは手の形をしており，ビジターはアメリカ式に握手をしてから店内に入るという趣向になっている。
また，照明，家具，什器，ブロンズの造作，グラスファイバー製の金色に塗られたサボテンの装飾などもすべて，かれのデザインによるもので，かれのかかえる専門職人に依頼してアメリカで作られ，日本で最後の仕上げがなされたオリジナルなものである。

SURF'N TURF
Pop art in 60s' became popular mainly in the states and the U.K., using mass media such as newspapers and TV in parodic or satirical way to create or re-discover new value. This art movement influenced a various field of culture and the formed pop culture.
Using American cartoonish style, Jordan Mozer designed this exciting restaurant in Matsuyama city. The design is playful and joyful. Door handles, for example, have hand shapes, so visitors are to do American way hand shaking before he or she enter the restaurant.
Mozer designed himself lighting, furniture, decorations, bronze objects, glass fiber golden cacti, an other details, collaborating with artists in America and they were finally completed in Japan.

1

禁酒法時代がテーマの郊外型アミューズメントレストラン

FBI

熊本県熊本市佐土原2丁目5-135

Amusement Restaurant FBI

Sadohara Kumamoto-shi Kumamoto
Designer KEIJI MITSUYAMA

設計／汎建築設計事務所＋丹青社
　　光山惠治　三輪幸夫　夏山孝博　藤原正一郎
協力／構造　光山進治　厨房　サッポロライオン
　　壁面制作　池田シューコウ
施工／井関建設＋松村組

1. 東側外観。夜間はライトアップされて印象度を強める
East view from the parking area
2. バーベキュー・コーナーよりブリッジを通して2階客席を見る
2F: Whole view of the well and bridge from the barbecue area

2

FBI 1F PLAN 1:400

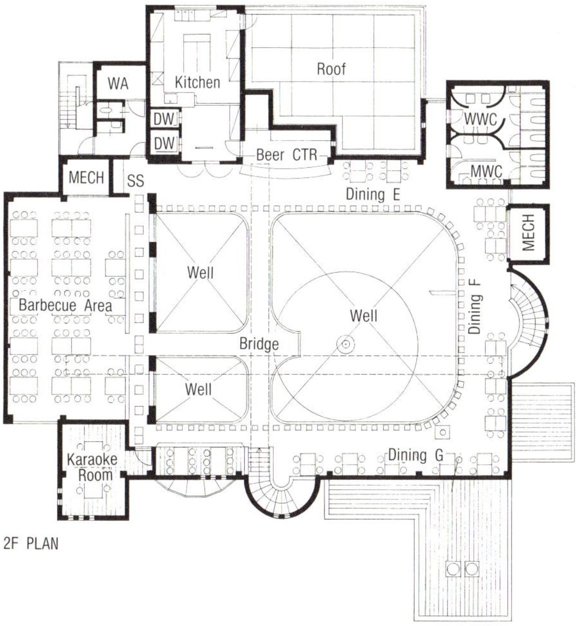

2F PLAN

●巨大なビアタンクの創り出す世界
禁酒法時代というのはローリングトウェンティとよばれた1920年代のアメリカを指す。シカゴ・ギャングたちが我が物顔に暴れまわった揺れ動く時代をテーマにこの郊外型レストランは企画された。
九州の中央にある熊本市と熊本空港を結ぶ幹線道路に面したレンガ積みの外装は，新築にもかかわらず古レンガを使用し，目地も特殊な処理をすることにより歳月を感じさせる仕上げとなっている。また，夜間にはライトアップされた外観がくっきりと夜空に浮かび上がり，疾走するカードライバーに強い印象をあたえる。
内部空間を決定づけているのは直径約８メートルの大きさを持つ本物のビアタンク（ビールの煮沸釜）である。世界最大のこのビアタンクは実際にサッポロビール恵比寿工場で稼動していたものであり，赤銅色に光る巨大なフォルムは，いかにも禁酒法時代の密造工場をイメージさせ，来客を別世界へと運んでくれる。

3. ビアタンクをそのまま活用した1階中央客席
View of the beer tank seatings

FBI
Design concept of this urban restaurant is Prohibition and Roaring Twenties when Chicago mobs made terrible havocs on streets.
A brick building in front of highway connecting Kumamoto city, the central city in Kyushu Island, and the Kumamoto airport. Old bricks and traditional joint technique were used for the exterior brick work to express an authentic appearance. When the building is lit up at night, it will give a strong impression to drivers running at full speed on the highway.
The most impressive interior element is an 8m diameter beer boiler and it was the biggest in the world and used before in Ebisu factory of Sapporo Breweries, Ltd. in Tokyo. The huge brown salvage tank remind us of an atmosphere of Prohibition and it would take us to the imaginary world at that time.

3

1

ハリウッド映画をテーマにしたアメリカンレストラン

ルドルフ・バーベキュー

大阪府大阪市中央区西心斎橋１丁目10-14

Restaurant RUDOLPHS BAR·B·QUE

Nishi-shinsaibashi Chuo-ku Osaka
Designer Sampei Abe

設計／シチュエーション　安部讃平
協力／建築実施設計　伊藤進郎建築設計事務所　伊藤進郎
施工／創美　石田英男

1. 道路側から正面ファサード夜景　**Night view of the facade from the street side**
2. 大きな樹が中央に植えられた1階パティオ客席　**1F: View of the patio from the garden**

2

3

●中庭のある居心地の良い倉庫
アメリカのレストランチェーンが国外にフランチャイズ展開するとき，メニューや味，オペレーションシステムだけでなく，デザインイメージも統一されている場合が多い。大阪・心斎橋に5年間の期限付きで建てられたこの仮設店舗は，アメリカにある同名のレストランのフランチャイジーであるが，デザインは違うものとなっている。
建物の外観はニューヨークのソーホーにある倉庫を思わせる古レンガ貼りで，内部はハリウッド映画のポスターなどを配した若者向きのカジュアルなデザインとされた。内部空間を特徴づけているのは，店内中央に設けられたパティオで，上部が吹き抜けた開放的な空間に一本の大きな木が植えられている。昼間はトップライトから太陽光が差し込み，この界隈には珍しい自然を感じさせる居心地の良い空間を，空気のように軽やかに客が行き来する。また，吹き抜けを囲む形で配された2階の客席は，三つのコーナーに分けられ，パーティールームとしても使用できる。

3. 厨房入り口側から見た1階パティオと通路
1F: View of the patio from the corridor

RUDOLPHS BAR.B.QUE
In most cases, when American chain restaurants go abroad to develop their franchise, they unify menus, flavors, operation systems, design, and atmosphere. However, this temporary American franchised restaurant with 5 years limited lease was exceptionally designed out of standard.
The brick work exterior reminds us of a N.Y. Soho warehouse and the interior was designed casually, using Hollywood movie posters, to target young people. The central patio with a top light and a big plant in the center accentuates the space impressively. In the daytime, visitors ramble freely, as is rarely in this area.
The second floor's seats are arranged to surround the void, and there are three areas to hold parties.

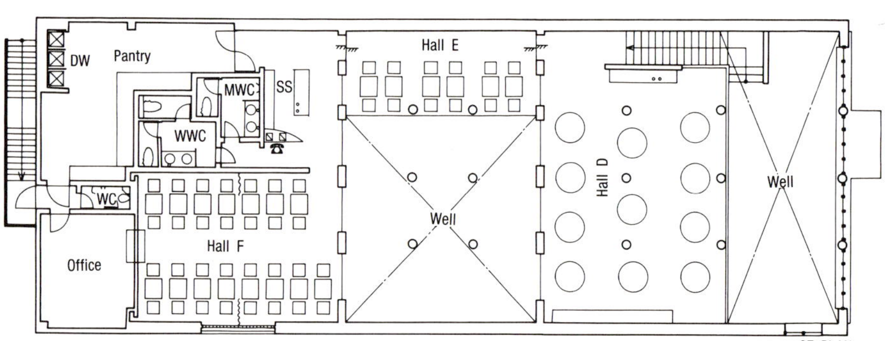

2F PLAN

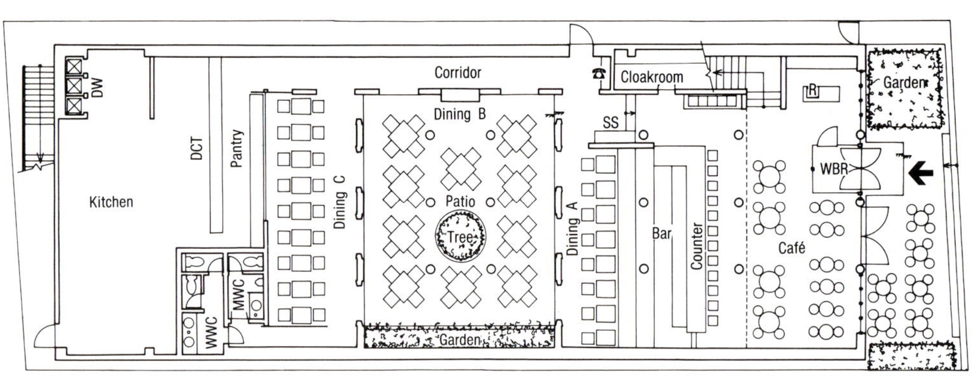

RUDOLPHS 1F PLAN 1:300

夜間はパブとなるオフィスビルのランチレストラン

ファミール シナネン店

東京都品川区東品川1-39 シナネンカナルサイドビル地下1階

設計/YMデザインパートナーズ 笠井三笠 佐藤貴光
施工/大明工芸

Dining & Cafe FAMIL Shinanen

Higashi-shinagawa Shinagawa-ku Tokyo, Designer YM Design Partners

1. 客席Bの陰影を強調した柱形デザイン
View of the dining B from the bar corner

1

●海の静寂さと荒々しさがテーマ
東京のウオーターフロントに面する天王洲は流通倉庫街であったが，近年，モノレールの駅ができたことにより巨大なオフィスビルが次々と建てられ，一大ビジネス街へと変貌しつつある。このレストランは新しく建てられたビルの地下1階にあり，昼間は上階に勤めるビジネスマンを対象にランチを提供，夜間は酒も飲めるパブとして企画された。
空間のデザインは，極端な静けさと強い荒々しさの共存，緊張と動きに満ちた内的な世界がテーマであった。そのために色と形によって表現された自然，特に海の表情を空間で体験できることが意図された。自然には，特に海には限定できない多くの表情があり，その有機的な，いかにも躍動的な姿を色とフォルムでイメージさせることにより，テーマが具現化できると考えられた。海底の岩を思わせる不規則な凹凸のつけられた天井や柱形，波のようにうねったフォルムを持つ照明柱の反射板やソファの背もたれ，そして，赤茶色の沈んだ色彩が不思議な静寂さと，荒々しさの予兆を感じさせる空間を造り出している。

2. 照明ポールの立ち並ぶ奥客席D内部
View of the dining D and lighting pole
3. 店内中央のバーコーナーを客席Bより見る
View of the bar from the dining B

FAMIL
Tennozu was an area of warehouses, facing Tokyo bay. Now with the open of the monorail station and rush of new buildings, it is developing and changing into a business district. This restaurant is located in the basement of a new building. It was planed to attract business people in the daytime, catering for their lunch, and at night providing a pub space for them.
The main theme of the interior design was a combination of something static and dynamic. It was a spiritual world of tension and movements. The designer tried to create

2

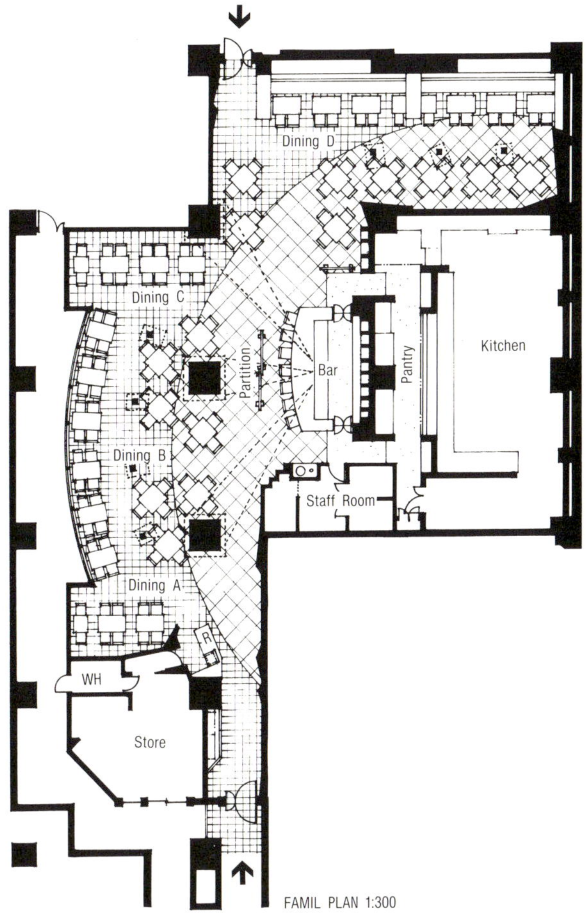

FAMIL PLAN 1:300

a space for visitors to experience the nature, particularly expressions of the sea.
He pondered how to express unlimited expressions of the sea and how to give them lively colors and forms to embody the leitmotif.
Uneven ceiling and columns, whiplash forms of light supports, reflector, and sofa back, all make us feel like we were at the bottom of the sea. Besides, reddish brown color helps to create an atmosphere filled with strangely quietness and precursor of something violent.

3

多目的ホールと複合したシアターレストラン

インコントロ

東京都世田谷区玉川3丁目17-1
玉川高島屋SC西館1階

Ristorante Italiano l'INCONTRO

Tamagawa Setagaya-ku Tokyo
Designer Norihiko Dan

企画／東神開発
設計／團・青島建築設計事務所
　團 紀彦　八木佐千子
協力　設備　日立プラント建設
　音響　音響シアターテック　石井浩美
　照明　フランケンズカムパニー　行田 彰
　テーブルウエア　テーブルギャラリー
施工　日産建設・日昌建設共同企業体
　高島屋建装事業部

●二重三重の役割を果たす空間形態
ショッピングセンターの駐車場ビルを部分的に改装したこのレストランは，隣にあるエキシビションホールと一体化したデザインで構成されている。外部道路からアプローチ通路を入った突き当たりがホールの入り口であり，その右側にレストランのロビーが広がる。ホールで催しが行われている時は，レストランがホワイエの役割を果たすと同時に，内部空間にも搬出入のために両者をつなぐ連絡口が設けられている。
レストラン内部の特徴は，1階レベルのロビーから中地下レベルの客席へ至る階段が広くとられ，そこが円環状のスクリーンが配された ステージとなっていることである。隣のホールとは別に，このレストランでは階段ステージを利用して定期的にライブイベントやコンサートが開かれている。周囲の高級住宅地に住む人々は，イタリア料理を味わいながらライブコンサートを楽しむことができるのである。

1. 中央客席Aより階段状のステージ方向を見る
View of the stair stage from the dining A

l'INCONTRO
Renovated partly from a car parking space of a shopping mall, this restaurant includes an adjacent exhibition hall. Entering from the door of the ground floor, visitors go through a hallway to entrance to the hall. On the right there is a lobby of the restaurant, which is used as a foyer or sort of buffer zone between the interior space and passage for carrying in and out something for the exhibition hall.
The characteristics of the interior is a big stairs with an encircled stage surrounded by columns arranged in a circle.
As well as the neighboring hall, this circle stage offers a live performance or events. Neighbors living in a near upper-class residents come here to dine Italian food, enjoying live stage performances.

1

2

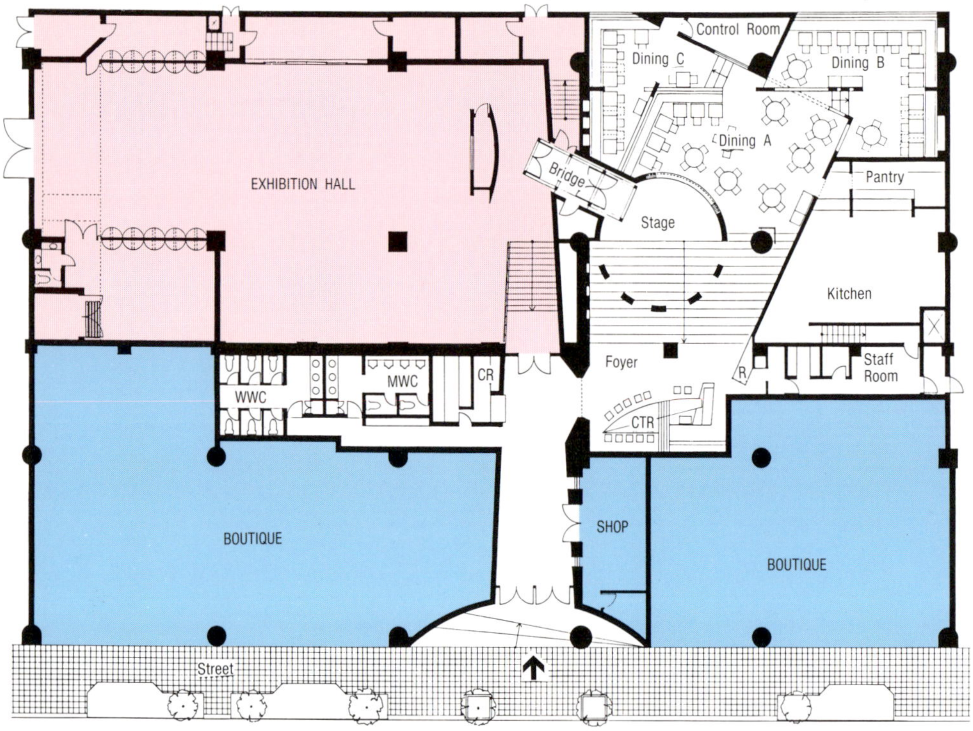

I'INCONTRO PLAN 1:400

2. 客席Aより客席C方向を見る **View of the dining A and bridge**

ハイグレードな雰囲気の洋風懐石レストラン

つかしげ

大阪府東大阪市下小坂２丁目７－８　ハイツウエムロ１階

設計／フレスコ　足立和夫　戸田守長
施工／布谷

Kaiseki Restaurant TSUKASHIGE

Shimokosaka Higashi-osaka-shi Osaka, Designer Kazuo Adachi

1. 入り口から奥方向へ延びる中央通路を見る
View of the center corridor from the entry side

1

2

●視点の移動により表情の変わる空間

人は座ったり，立ち上がったり，通り過ぎたりすることにより眼の視点が変わり，風景が少しずつ変化していく。大阪郊外にある住宅地の一角にできたこのレストランは，アイレベルの変化による空間の表情の変化を，より効果的に表現することがデザインのコンセプトとされた。

内部空間に使用される素材は，見る角度が少しでも変わると表情が一変するものが選ばれ，たとえば，ポリエステルファイバーを細かく編み上げたスクリーンは二重に重ねることにより，微妙に変化するモアレ模様を生み出す。中央のメーン通路両側に配された異形のオブジェ柱も，見る角度によってまったく異なる風景を造り出す重要なエレメントである。また，外光を通したベネチアングラスの色彩は内部の照明と相まって，時間の経過により同じ場所でも違う印象を与え，入り口から連続するパースペクティブな風景に多様さをもたらしている。

TSUKASHIGE

Our viewpoints vary by our postures. Sitting, standing, and moving, we change our scopes. This restaurant in a residential area of a suburb of Osaka uses the effect of eye level to change our views as a part of design concept.

The interior materials were carefully chosen to display manifold textures from different angles. For example, intricate polyester

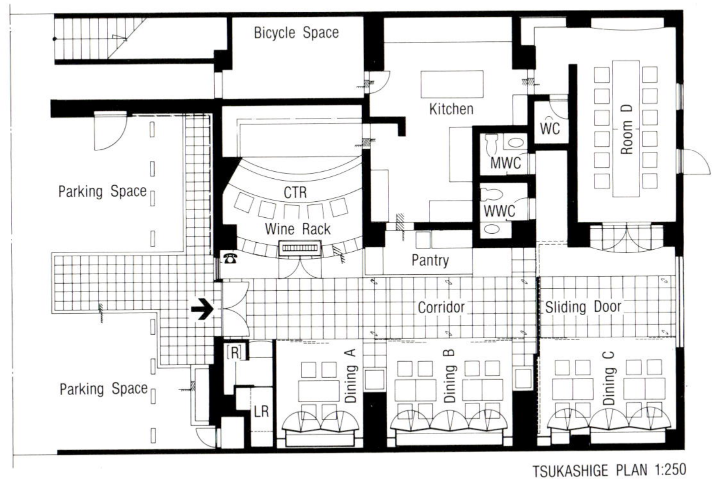

TSUKASHIGE PLAN 1:250

2. 個室D入り口側から中央通路ごしに見た客席Cと客席B
View of the dining C and B from the room D
3. ステンドグラスにより表情の変化する個室A内部
View of the room D and stained glass windows

3

meshes show moire effect patterns when they are used layers. The main corridor has decorative slim spindle-shaped columns on both sides look different from seers' eye levels.

Sunlight through a Venetian glass window, with the interior light give us various impression, depending when and where we see it, so the perspective view from the entrance appears interesting and diverse.

和食と洋食を複合させた郊外型ファミリーレストラン

グルメドーム

大阪府南河内郡美原町青南台１丁目1197-773

Restaurant GOURMET DOME

Mihara-cho Minami-kawachi-gun Osaka, Designer Masaki Nitta

1

2

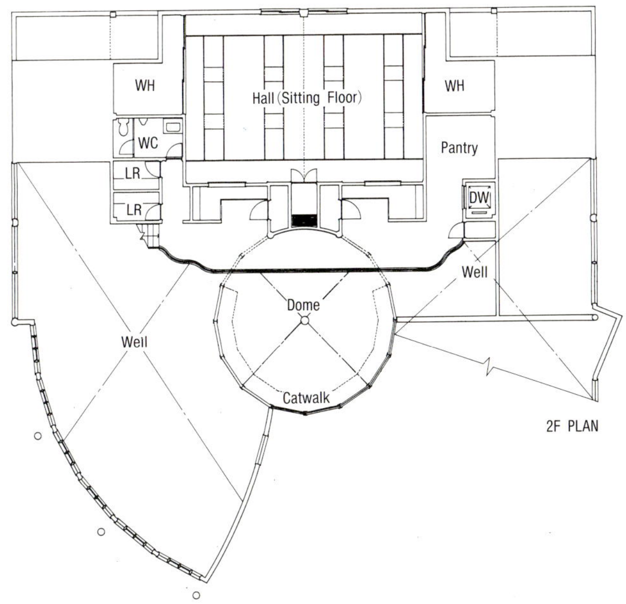

2F PLAN

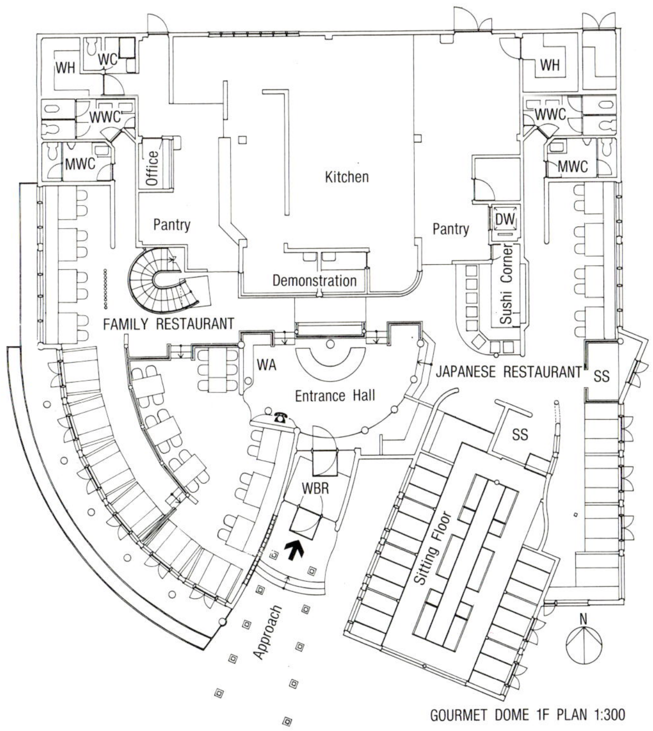

GOURMET DOME 1F PLAN 1:300

設計／新田正樹建築設計工房
協力／サン設計　南都設計　アサヒ設備
施工　峯工務店

1. 道路側から見た南側正面外観。中央が入り口
South view from the street side
2. キャンバス張りのドーム天井部分を見る
View of the dome from the entrance hall

3

●ドームにより和と洋の客席を分割

均一な味とサービスを売りものにしたファミリーレストランチェーンは，出現以来そのリーズナブルな価格と親しみ易さにより日本中を席巻してきた。しかし，その均一な味とデザインは次第に飽きられ，次の新しい展開が求められるようになってきた。

大阪の郊外にある木材工業団地の一角にできたこのロードサイドレストランは，洋食レストランと和食レストランを複合させることにより，新しいタイプのファミリーレストランを出現させようとしたものである。

店名を象徴するエントランスホール上部のドームはテント張りで，高窓の開口部と共に自然光を内部空間に満たし，開放的ではあるが非日常的な印象を来客に与える。ドームはまた，内部を洋風レストランと和食レストランに分ける役割を持っており，左側がイス席だけの洋食コーナー，右側がタタミ席とイス席を組み合わせた和食コーナーという構成になっている。

3. ファミリーレストラン客席を2階より見る
View of the family restaurant
4. 和食コーナーの掘り込み席全景
View of the sitting floor corner

GOURMET DOME

With their uniformed taste and service, a series of chain family restaurants became very popular throughout Japan and the people enjoy their low prices and friendly atmosphere. However, it seems that customers are gradually getting tired of the stereotyped food and the interiors, and food business is asked to innovate new types or styles.

Opened in an area of a wood factory complex, this road side restaurant was planned to combine Western and Japanese styles to create a new type family restaurant.

As its name tells, it has a dome tent on the top. The sunshine comes from the dome and the vertical openings and fill the total space. It looks open and somewhat surrealistic. The dome also functions to divide space into Western food area and Japanese.

The former has chairs and tables and the latter has a tatami seating area and tables with chairs.

4

スノーパークのためのレストハウス&レストラン

オプスおぐに

新潟県刈羽郡小国町大字上岩田208

Rest House O·P·S OGUNI

Oguni-machi Kariha-gun Niigata, Designer Kikoo Mozuna

設計／毛綱毅曠建築事務所　毛綱毅曠　水谷不二男　石川由紀子　斎藤彰宏
サインデザイン／毛綱毅曠建築事務所　水谷不二男
協力／構造設備　細貝建築事務所
施工／清水建設北陸支店

1. スノーモビル用ゲレンデから見た外観夜景
Night view from the snowmobile slope

1

2

●雪国のランドマーク

リゾート地には，シーズン型と通年型の2タイプがある。シーズン型は対象となる季節しか客は来ないが，通年型は季節に応じたリゾートの楽しみ方ができるよう工夫されている。雪の多い新潟地方の小国町には広大な森林公園があり，春から秋のグリーンシーズンには多くの客が訪れるが，冬には客がほとんどこない。

地域振興のため，冬場にも客が訪れるようにスキーのためのミニゲレンデ，スノーモービルを使ったウインタースポーツなどが企画され，その中心施設として企画されたのがこのレストハウス兼レストランである。地域のランドマークとなるようにカラフルな外装を施された建築は，1階がエントランスホールとスノーモビルの格納庫，タワー状の上階は2階が厨房，3階がレストラン，4階がカフェというフロア構成となっている。

デザインのモチーフは，この地方では「へんなか」とよばれるイロリで，1階中央には暖炉がそのシンボルとして鎮座している。

2. タワーの入り口まわり外観
View of the tower from the corridor
3. タワー1階入り口ホール中央のイロリ
View of the fireplace from the entry

O.P.S OGUNI

Resort areas have two types: seasonal and all-year-round resorts. The former attract visitors only in the season but the latter can welcome visitors any season with their facilities.

Oguni-cho in heavily snowy Niigata prefecture has a vast forest park and it gathers a lot of tourists from spring to summer, but almost none in winter.

To re-vitalize local economy and to attract people even in winter, the town built small ski slopes, snow mobile slopes, and this rest house and restaurant as the center of facilities.

As a local landmark, the exterior is colorfully painted. The first floor is entrance a hall and a garage for snow mobiles, the second tower floor kitchen, the third a restaurant , and the fourth floor a cafe. The design concept was based upon "hennaka" a local style hearth, which was symbolically expressed by a fireplace in the center of the first floor.

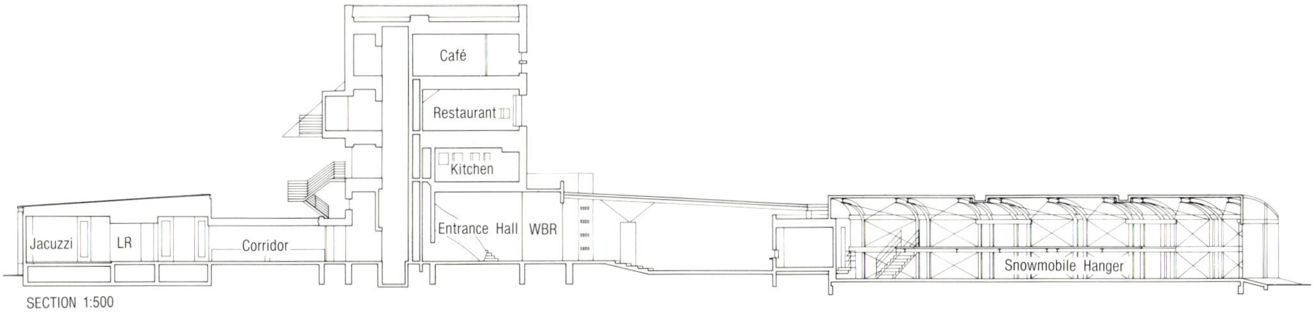
Café
Restaurant
Kitchen
Jacuzzi
LR
Corridor
Entrance Hall
WBR
Snowmobile Hanger
SECTION 1:500

3

4

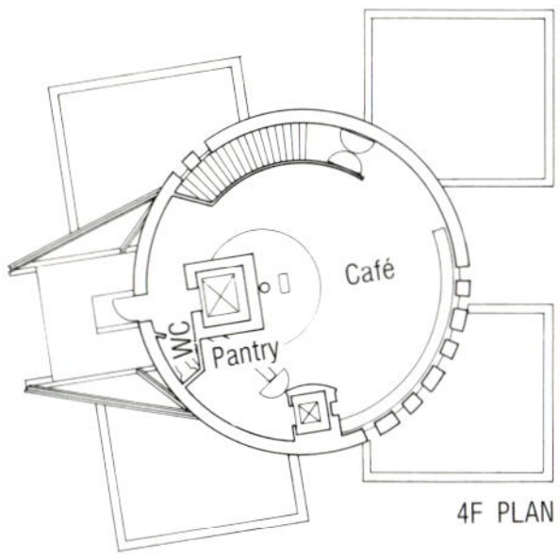

4F PLAN

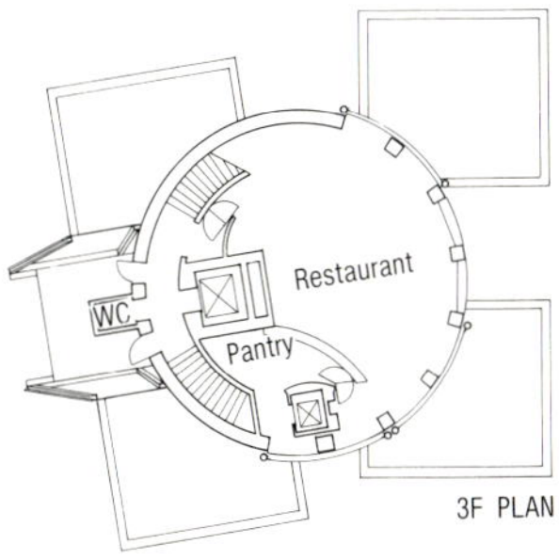

3F PLAN

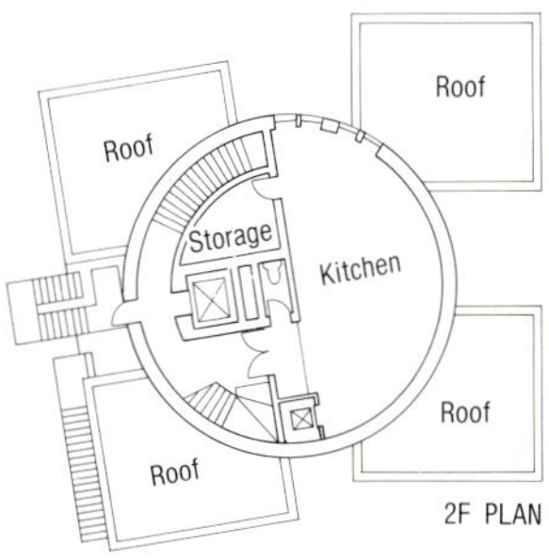

2F PLAN

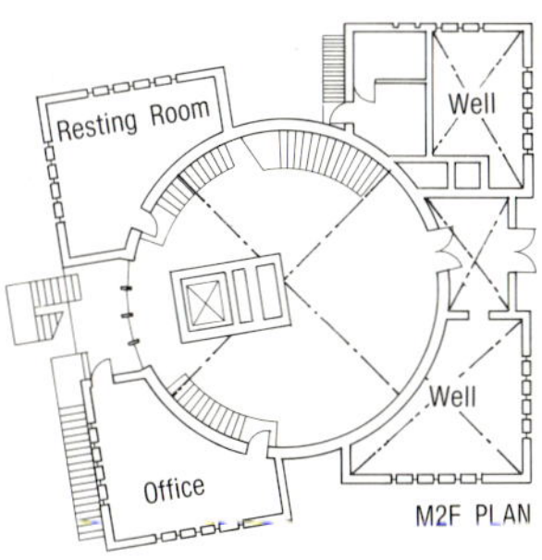

M2F PLAN

5

4. タワー4階のカフェ内部客席を暖炉側より見る
4F: View of the cafe from the fireplace
5. タワー3階のレストラン内部窓側客席
3F: View of the restaurant interior

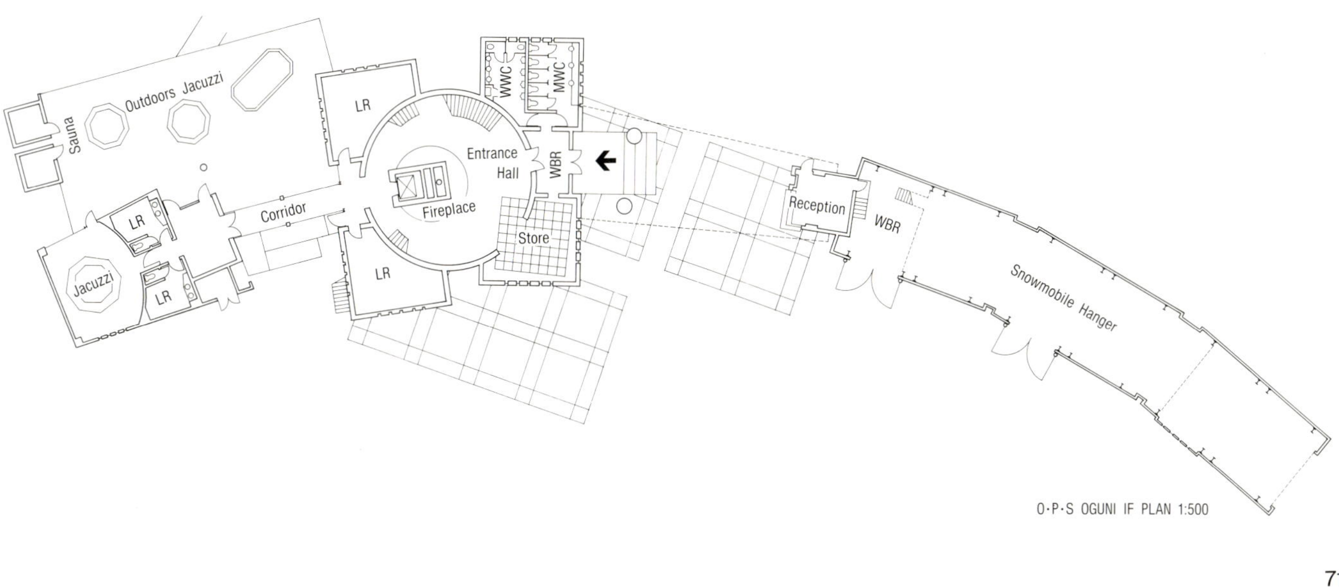

O·P·S OGUNI IF PLAN 1:500

海と丘が見渡せる美術館内のレストラン

里蘇

静岡県伊東市富戸字水口1101 伊豆高原美術館２階

Restaurant RISO

Futo Ito-shi Shizuoka
Designer Ryuji Takenaga

企画／然建築研究所　嵐山浩志
設計／然建築研究所　武長龍二　園原一代　岩渕純子
施工／チカル工芸

1. カウンター席より屋外に広がる海と丘の自然を見る
View of the sea and hill from the counter
2. レジわきから見た中央客席A全景。海に浮かぶ島のイメージ
View of the dining A from the cashier side

1

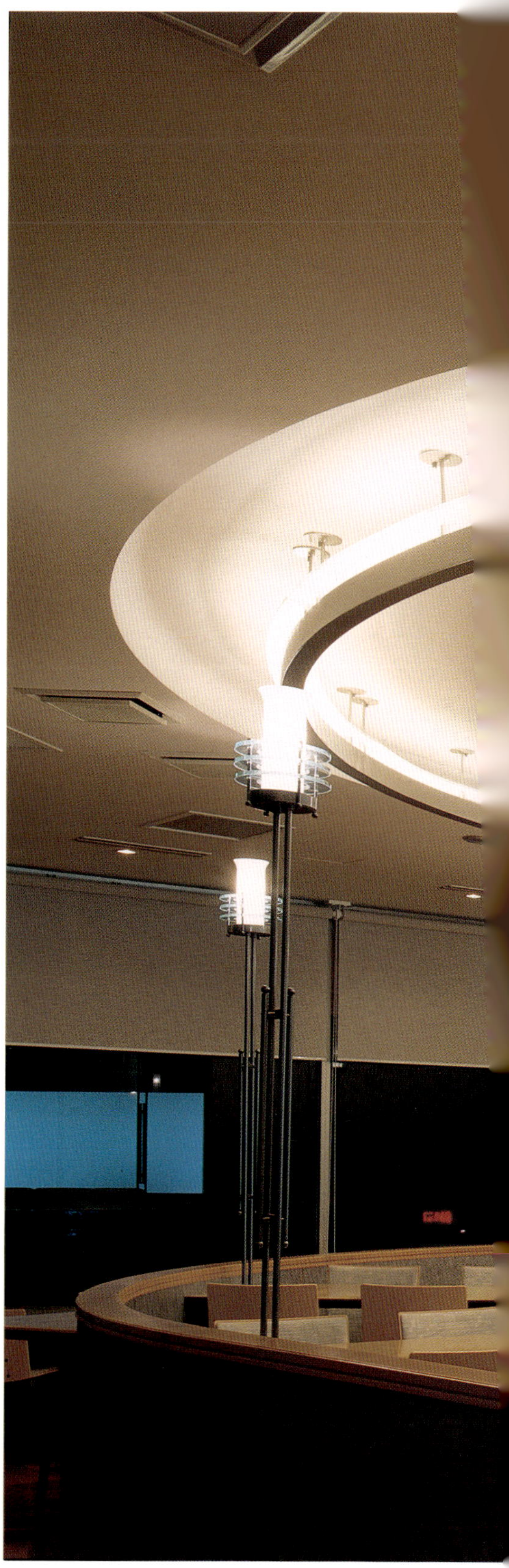

●外部の自然を深く感受できるデザイン

欧米では美術館にレストランが併設されることは珍しくないが，日本では，まだその例は少ない。伊豆半島の観光地・伊東市にできたこのレストランは，江戸時代の版画や絵画の展示をメーンとした美術館内部に併設されたものであり，デザインも美術館と同じ設計者が手掛けた。

海が遠望できる小高い丘の上にあるため，周囲の素晴らしい眺望と豊かな自然を生かし，どのように表現するかが設計の最大のポイントとなった。海に面した２面の

2

壁は床から天井までガラス張りの開口部とされ，また奥の楕円形のパーティションに囲まれた客席は床レベルが上げられて，野外の景色を楽しめるように配慮されている。
インテリアの素材も，海だけではなく，前景に広がる丘陵地の緑を含めてのデザインということで，できるだけナチュラルな木の材質感を生かしたものとされた。また，奥の楕円形のパーティションに囲まれた客席は，沖に浮かぶ島，あるいは船になぞらえてデザインされたものである。

RISO
Western museums often has refined restaurants but Japanese ones seldom. Displaying wood prints and Japanese paintings of Edo era, this museum in a resort city Ito in Izu peninsula has a splendid restaurant. Both the museum and the restaurant was designed by the same architect.
The architect planed to make most use of surroundings and the view, for the museum site was on the top of a high hill and commands a fine view of the sea. The sea side two openings were glazed from the floor to the ceiling. A dining area encircled by oval partition had a rise for people to enjoy nice scenery. This area is designed upon an image of an island.
As for the interior material, natural wood is mostly used to fit both the sea and the green of the hill.

3

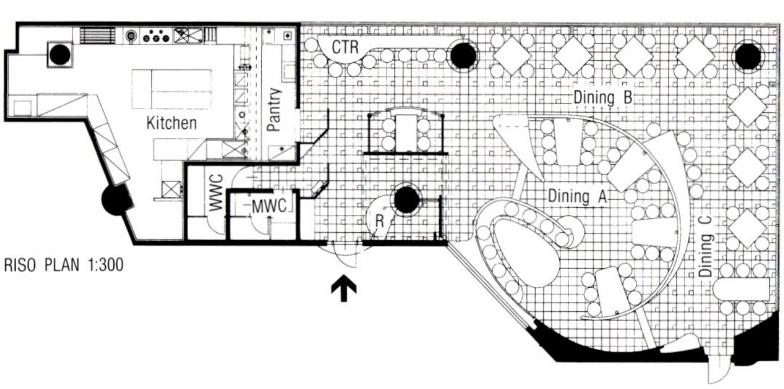

3. 中央客席Aを奥の客席Cより見る　**View of the dining A from the dining C**

BEER RESTAURANTS & STEAK RESTAURANTS

アートと一体化したビジネス街のビアレストラン

クリスタルコート

大阪府大阪市中央区城見1丁目2-27
OBPクリスタルタワー地下1階

Beer Restaurant
CRYSTAL COURT

Shiromi Chuo-ku Osaka
Producer Fujio Maeyama

企画／目玉企画　前山富士雄
設計／アイディーエス企画　岡田敦子
協力／ガラス&スチールオブジェ　ダニー・レーン
施工／竹中工務店

●ヨーロッパ文化の中のモダンならざるもの
ビールはヨーロッパから伝わってきたものであり，ビアホールといえばイギリスのパブ，ドイツのビアハウスをイメージさせるデザインのものがほとんどである。大阪の新しく開発されつつあるビジネス街の，巨大なオフィスビル地下1階にあるこの大型ビアレストランは，さらに時代をさかのぼり，ヨーロッパ文化の中の“モダンならざる”ものをデザインのコンセプトとしている。
コンセプトを実現するため，空間のいっそうのオブジェ化が進められ，具体的な方法としてイギリスでガラス工芸を学んだアメリカ人，ダニー・レーンが起用された。ガラスの魔術師とよばれる彼のつくったオブジェは，入り口ホールの中央に鎮座し，積層されてラセン形に彫り込まれたガラス柱が独特の質感を発散し，場の空気を決定づけている。
また，奥にあるバーカウンターは長さ37メートル余りもある長大なもので，その直線的なフォルムは，布や曲面状のスチールオブジェによる有機的ラインと対比され，空間にバランスをもたらしている。

1. 入り口ゲートより見たホール中央のガラスオブジェ
View of the glass object from the gate

CRYSTAL COURT
British pubs and German beer halls have been models for most beer restaurants in Japan, since beer was introduced to this country from the West.
This beer restaurant in the basement of a gigantic office building in newly-developing business area in Osaka was designed to abandon both traditional European style and modernistic one.
The design concept came from something of anti-modernism in European culture. The result was a space as one artistic object.
Danny Lane, an American artist, who studied glass art in the U.K., joined this project. Called "a magician of glass art", he created work in the center of the entrance hall. It is a big screw-shaped layered glass plates, showing itself as a beautiful translucent mass to make an unusual atmosphere in the interior.
A 37m long straight counter in the back, together with fabrics and curved steel objects, makes interesting contrast between organic and inorganic lines of the design.

1

2

3

2. 有機的なラインをえがく入り口右側の客席E
View of the dining E from the Hall
3. 中央にビアサーバーを持つ37mの長大なカウンター席
View of the long counter from the dining D

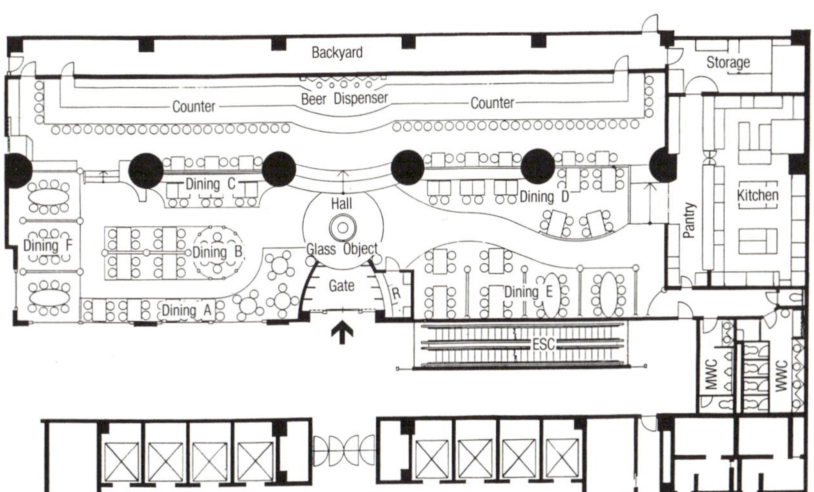

CRYSTAL COURT PLAN 1:400

メリケン波止場の夜景を生かした大型ビアレストラン

クイクイ

兵庫県神戸市中央区東川崎町１丁目６－１　高浜モザイク２階

Beer Restaurant QUI QUI

Higashikawasaki-cho Chuo-ku Kobe, Producer Fujio Maeyama

1

企画／ユリイカ　前山富士雄　門 浩志　設計／クマクリエイト　野下達雄
協力／音響　サウンドプロセスデザイン　岩井利信
照明計画　松下電工　野田高季
空調計画　阪急百貨店建装部　中村哲司
施工／阪急百貨店建装部　大羽慶徳

1. 入り口ホールの照明オブジェを客席への通路より見る
View of the entrance hall from the approach corridor

●文明を通過し離脱していくエトランゼ
高浜モザイクは，神戸のウオーターフロントにある神戸ハーバーランドの商業施設ビルであり，メリケン波止場を望む海の眺望が売りものである。ビルの２階にあるこの大型ビアレストランは立地の魅力をフルに生かすため，海に面したガラス張りの開口部に長さ50メートルの長大なカウンターが配されている。
デザインのテーマは，イスタンブールというイスラムとヨーロッパの二重文明に育まれた都市。文明を通過し，離脱していくエトランゼのように，この都市を出発して地図のない場所へとモチーフは展開していく。「バザール」「アヤソフィア」，「砂漠の幕舎」のコーナーは，ネーミングをイメージさせるデザインであっても，それらを具体的に再現したものではなく，幻をなぞりつつ来客を不思議な世界へと導いてくれる。
今日も，若い女性を中心とした客たちは，メリケン波止場の美しい夜景を見ながら，日常性から切り離された別世界の夢にひたるのである。

QUI QUI
The Takahama Mosaic is a commercial complex of the Kobe Harbor Land in water-front area of Kobe, Hyogo. Commanding "Meriken (American) harbor" of the Kobe port, this big restaurant is located on the second floor of a building and has a 50m long window side counter to make the most of the splendid view of the sea.
Design theme is Istanbul, a city where Islamic culture meets European one. The interior was like a mental image of a stranger that traveled and passing through various cultures. The leitmotif was developed from Istanbul to somewhere we could not find in any maps.
"Bazzar", "Ayasophia", "Tents On The Desert" are names of dining areas and each design is not just the mimicry but something mysterious, taking guests to imaginary travel to the world of wonder.
Today here, visitors, mostly young women, are lost in their daydream of another surreal world, seeing a wonderful view of "Meriken harbor".

2

2. 客席Aの壁面上部に描かれた壁画　**The mural paintings of the dining A**
3. 客席A中央の列柱と照明器具　**The columns of the dining A**

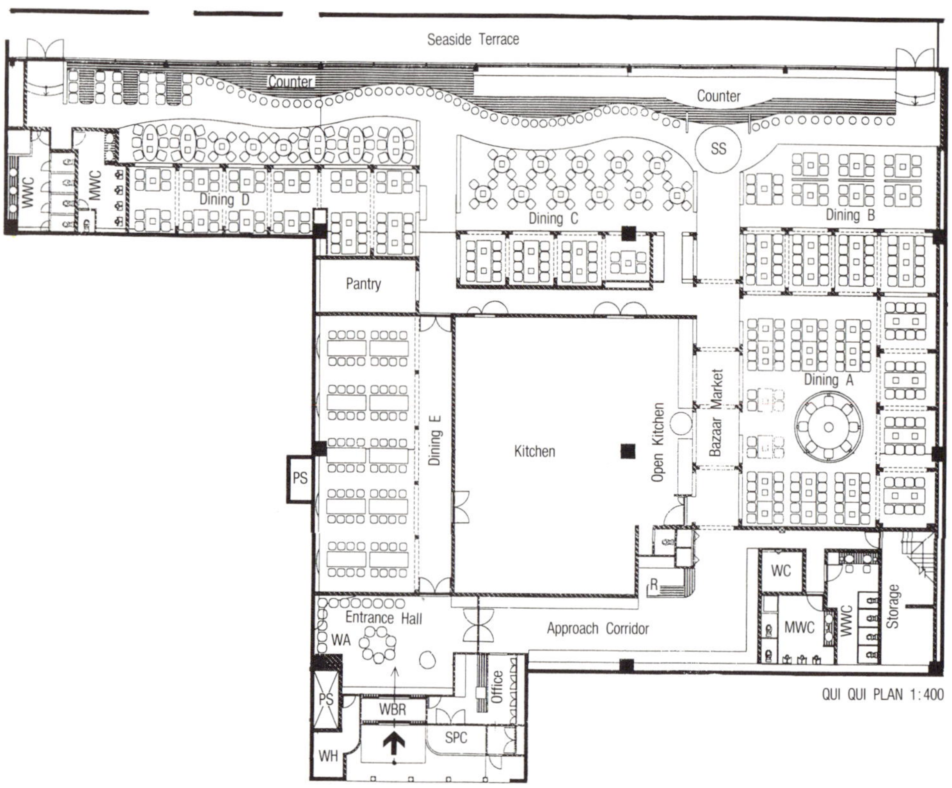

QUI QUI PLAN 1:400

3

124

ディスコから変身したビアレストラン

心斎橋倶楽部

大阪府大阪市中央区心斎橋筋２丁目１-19 延田ビル３・４階

Beer Restaurant SHINSAIBASHI CLUB

Shinsaibashi-suji Chuo-ku Osaka, Designer Sumio Yoshino

1

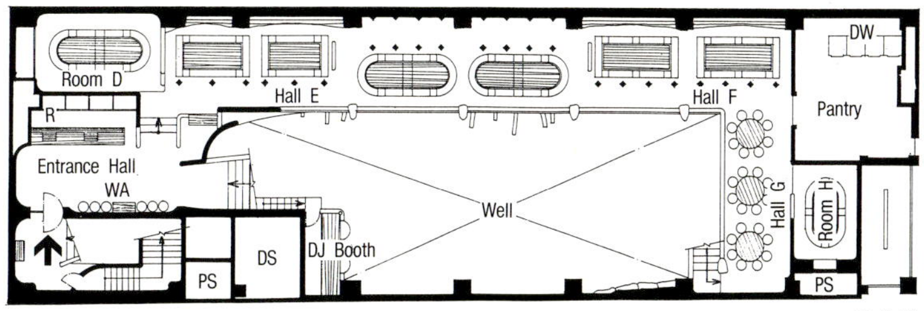

4F PLAN

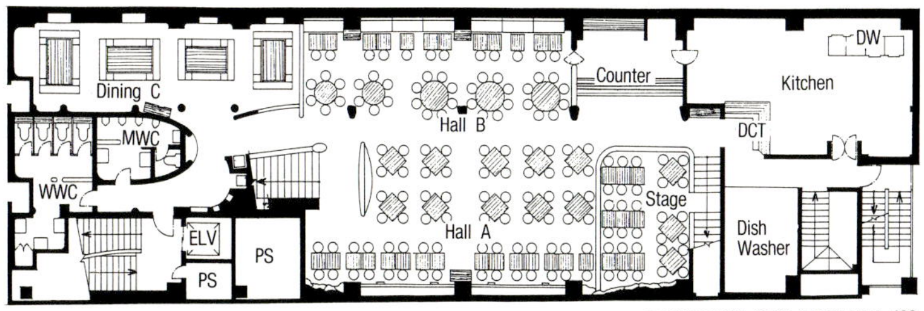

SHINSAIBASHI CLUB 3F PLAN 1:400

2

企画／エム・ディー　武藤豊彦
基本設計・デザイン／CSN　吉野純夫
設計／CSN　前田太郎　施工／トライ

1. 吹き抜けを通して3階客席を4階客席Fより見る
View of the third floor from the fourth floor
2. 入り口ホールから3階へ降りる階段まわり
View of the stairwell from the Hall B

C-2

4

●メキシカンリゾートがテーマ
ディスコ・ブームの去った後，その空いたスペースをどうするかは難しい問題である。ワンフロアの面積が大きい上に，ダンススペースや照明など特殊な設備が残されているからである。大阪・心斎橋にできたこのレストランは，ビルの3・4階を占めていたディスコを大型ビアホールへと巧みに変身させた例である。
デザインのテーマはメキシカンリゾートで，具体的にはサンタフェ風のスタイルが採り入れられ，ビアホールの陽気さと開放感を演出するためにカリブ的な雰囲気が付け加えられた。吹き抜け空間に置かれた高さ5メートルの巨大なサボテンやヤシの木，カラフルな土壁のスクリーンなどが，それらを表現している。また，ホリゾント風に壁の下部へ埋め込まれた照明が影絵のようにヤシの木を浮かび上がらせ，朝→夕方→夜という風に変化する照明パターンと相まって，都会の夜にひとときのリゾートスペースを提供している。

3

3. バンケットに使われる3階の客席C
3F: View of the dining C from the entry
4. ホリゾントに浮かび上がる3階ホール客席Aのヤシの木とサボテンのシルエット
3F: View of the cyclorama from the hall A

SHINSAIBASHI CLUB
After a disco boom in this country, there are a number of empty lots for owners to deal with immediately. It is not easy to renovate disco lots, since their sites are very wide and they have special facility, dance floor, special system lighting, etc.
This restaurant was renovated from a disco occupying the third and the fourth floor of a building in Shinsaibashi, Osaka. You see here a good remedy for disco lots or a smart example of changing a disco into a big beer hall.

Designed mostly upon Mexican resort style, plus some quotation from Santa Fe style and Caribbean atmosphere expressing openness and cheerfulness of tropical beer hall with 5m high palm trees, brilliantly colored walls. Built-in lamps and shadows of plants create tropical landscapes from morning till night. Here you enjoy a resort atmosphere even in a big city.

1

モニュメンタルな存在のビアレストラン

フラムドール

東京都墨田区吾妻橋１丁目25-１　アサヒビール吾妻橋ホール１・２階

Beer Hall LA FLAMME D'OR

Azumabashi Sumida-ku Tokyo, Designer Philippe Starck

設計／フィリップ・スタルク　設計協力／野沢　誠+ゲット(GETT)
施工／大林組・鹿島建設・東武谷内田建設J.V.

1. 下へいくに従って幅がせまくなる階段のデザイン
View of the stair from the second floor
2. 吹き抜けを通して2階通路より1階階段まわりを見る
View of the stair and dining D from the second floor

2

3

3. ゆるやかに壁面がカーブした1階客席Cを客席Bより見る
1F: View of the dining C from the dining B
4. 吹き抜けを通して1階客席Cを2階階段途中より見る
View of the well and dining C from the stair

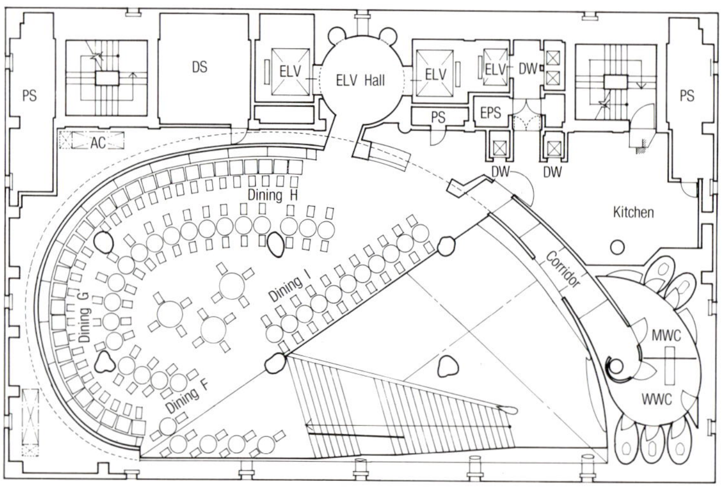

2F PLAN

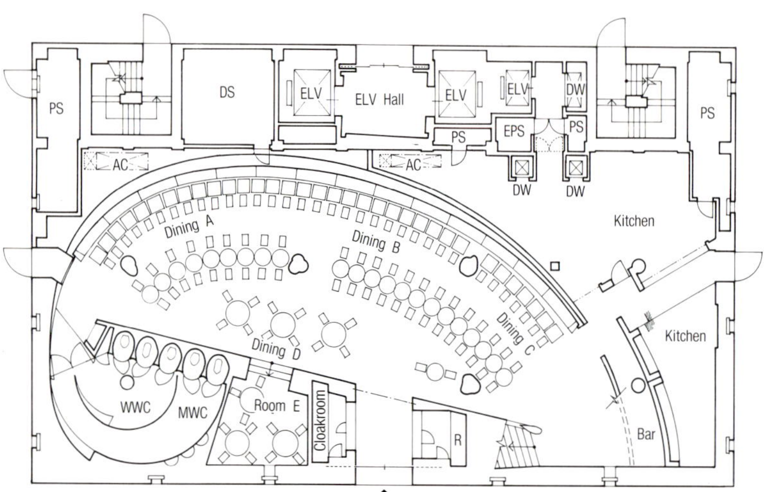

LA FLAMME D'OR 1F PLAN 1:300

●オブジェをスケールアウトした空間

浅草は，東京でもっとも下町らしい雰囲気のある地域であり，江戸時代からの風習を残している由緒ある町といえる。このビアホールのあるビルは浅草の隅田川に面した角地にあり，この地で永く工場を操業してきたビール会社が地域再開発を機会に建設したものである。浅草のもっとも目立つ場所にたてられたビルは，黒御影石で全面を覆われた彫刻的フォルムを持っており，屋上には炎をイメージした巨大な金色のオブジェが乗っている。あらゆる種類の雑多な建物やサイン広告に囲まれた環境の中で，どのデザインカテゴリーにも属さず，一度見たら忘れられないモニュメンタルな外観をというのがビルのコンセプトであり，内部のビアホールも同じ手法でデザインされた。

1・2階を貫く8本の構造柱は，ねじられたフランスパンをスケールアウトしたオブジェのようなユニークな形態を持ち，とても柱とは思えないデザインである。また，1・2階を結ぶ階段は上へ行くに従い，幅が3倍以上に広がり，視覚的なパースペクティブを錯覚させるなど，数々の斬新なデザインが展開されている。

LA FLAMME D'OR

Asakusa is one of towns in Tokyo, full of reminiscence of old things and customs since Edo period. Facing the Sumida River, this beer restaurant stands on a corner of Asakusa. It was planed as a re-development project for a beer brewery lot.

Located on a riverside and drawing people's attention, this sculptural building is fully covered with black granite and has a flame-like golden object on the top. Surrounded by buildings and signboards in different shapes and heights, this project remarkably keeps a high profile against ordinary architecture.

The impressive exterior was designed to be imprinted on onlookers' eyes at the first sight, and so was the interior.

Eight structural columns, designed like enlarged twisted French bread, going through the first and the second floor, are beyond our preconception for columns. The width of steps of a stairways connecting the first floor with the second floor are tripled from the lowest step to the top, creating a illusionary effect of its perspective. Besides the designer displayed a number of novel design elements and devices.

4

海鮮しゃぶをメーンとしたビアレストラン

しゃぶ鮮

東京都武蔵野市御殿山1丁目1-3
クリスタルパークビル地下1階

Shabu-Shabu Restaurant SHABU SEN

Gotenyama Musashino-shi Tokyo
Designer Shimpei Matsuki

企画／トレッドアソシエイツ
設計／松樹事務所ドメスティック
松樹秦平　勝又由美
施工／旭光

●冷と温, 洋と和のイメージを混交
ビールは基本的に夏の飲み物であり, 冷たい喉ごしの味が涼感を誘う。そして"しゃぶしゃぶ"は冬の鍋料理で, 温かさが体を包み込んでくれる。また, ビールは外国からきた"洋"のものであり, 鍋料理は日本古来の"和"のものである。
東京・吉祥寺のビル地下にできたこのビアレストランは, 二つの対比的な飲み物と料理を同時に組み合わせて提供することを企画のコンセプトとしている。しかし, デザインのテーマとしては, 両者のイメージを対比するのではなく, 折衷し混交することによって新しい魅力を生み出そうとした。
むき出しにされたままの建築のコンクリートスラブと天井は西洋的であるが, そこから吊り下げられたキャノピーに描かれた絵は日本的なモチーフであり, また, 壁の紅殻色の仕上げは伝統的な日本建築の手法であるが, 掛けられている絵は洋画である。空間の構成も中央の大テーブルのある大空間と, 細かく仕切ることのできる個室とが異和感なく連続するような工夫がなされている。

1. 大テーブル席とその上部を覆うキャノピー
View of the big table to the room A

SHABU SEN
No Japanese would deny that the best season for beer is summer, for they love to gulp beer as refreshments to enjoy feeling it passing through their throats. Shabu-shabu, boiling beef in pans, maybe most suitable for winter to warm ourselves. Beer was brought from the West and "nabe ryori", boiling food with a pan, is one of traditional Japanese foods. A good combination of the West and the East is the project concept.
This beer restaurant in a basement of a building in Kichijyoji was not planned to contrast the West and the East but to represent an attractive marriage of both culture as a sort of compromised proposal.
Exposed concrete slabs and ceiling are Western and the canopy-like drop ceiling has pictures of Japanese motifs. The finish treatment of red walls shows traditional Japanese architectural way.
The interior consists of a big area with a big table in the center and the another space is used, being divided into several rooms. Two areas fits successfully each other.

1

2

2. 奥の個室コーナーからダイニング客席方向を見る **View of the corridor from the room D**

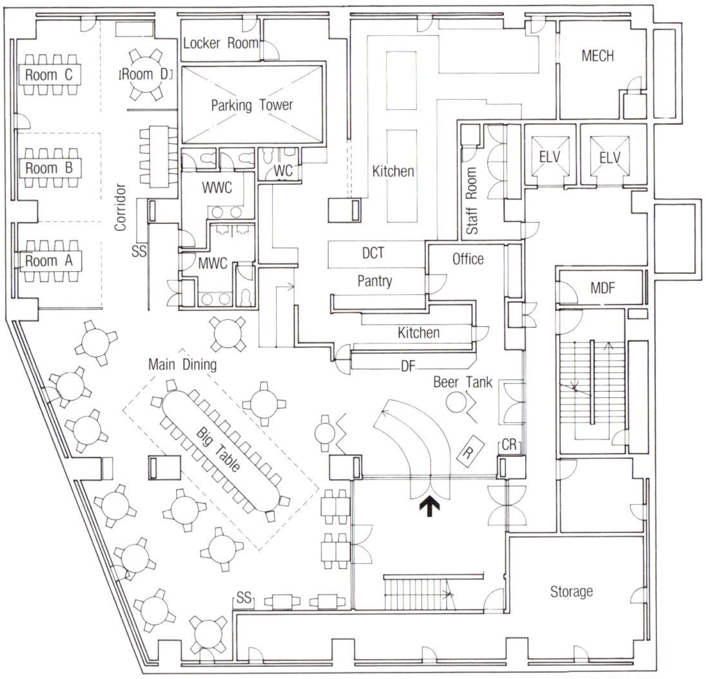

SHABU SEN PLAN 1:300

ビール倉庫の内部を改装したビアレストラン

キリン万代橋ホール

新潟県新潟市万代2丁目4-28

企画／新交企画　中野憲太
設計／浜野商品研究所　三島サトル
施工／建築　本間組　内装　シーエス新潟

Beer Hall KIRIN BANDAIBASHI HALL

Bandai Niigata-shi Niigata, Designer Satoru Mishima

1. ビール倉庫の一角を改装した入り口まわり夜景
Night view of the entry from the street side

1

2

●木格子が生み出す大陸のイメージ
日本海に面した新潟市は，海を渡ればロシアのウラジオストクと近い距離にあり，大陸との交流の歴史は古く，かつ長い。ソヴィエト連邦の崩壊した現在では，民間レベルでの経済交流が復活し，盛んに行われている。
新潟市の中央を流れる信濃川に架けられた万代橋。そのたもとにできたこのビアレストランは，ウラジオストクからさらに奥へ広がる満洲やシベリアなどの大陸内部をイメージしてデザインされた。古いビール倉庫の内部を改装した空間は，太く力強い建築の骨格をそのまま残して，木格子によるパネルをエレメントとして嵌め込むという手法がとられ，また，2 階のバンケットルームは，以前に使用されていたエレベーター室をそのまま流用したものである。
雪国らしく，奥に設けられた巨大なタワー状のストーブには薪がくべられ，また入り口わきのセイロからは白い蒸気が吹き上げられて，木格子の織りなす光と影が，温かく，そして力強い土のイメージ，すなわち大陸的なイメージを空間にもたらす。

KIRIN BANDAIBASHI HALL
Facing the Japan Sea, Niigata city is not far from Vladivostok over the sea and has the long history of interrelation between Japan and the Eurasia continent. After the corruption of the Soviet Union, economic relation between Japan and Eurasia re-opened and became active on private company level.
This beer restaurant is located near the Bandaibashi bridge over the Shinano River running through the center of the city.
Renovated from an old beer warehouse, the interior has wood lattices, leaving big structural columns as they were. On the second floor, an elevator room is used as a banquet room.
As the site is in snowy country, a big towering stove is put in the back and some pieces of wood are cracking in it as they burn.
White steam is rising from steamers near the entrance. Shadows of wood lattices give us a feeling of warmth of the Mother Earth of the Eurasia continent.

3

2. 店内奥の1階客席Bより薪ストーブごしに入り口方向を見る
1F: View of the firewood stove from the dining B
3. 業務用エレベーターのピットをそのまま利用した2階バンケットルーム
2F: View of the banquet room from the entry side

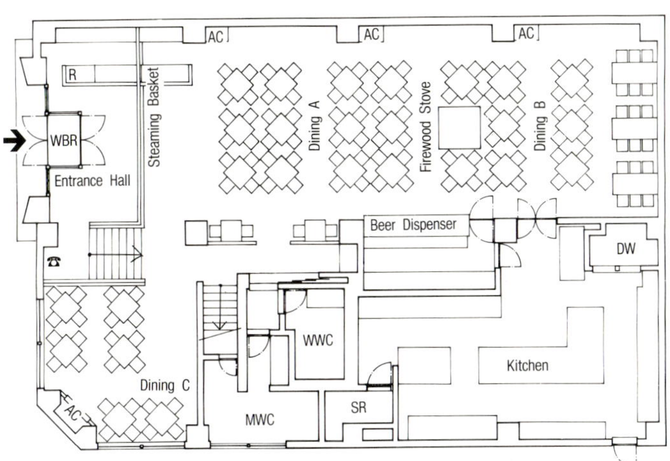

KIRIN BANDAIBASHI HALL 1F PLAN 1:250

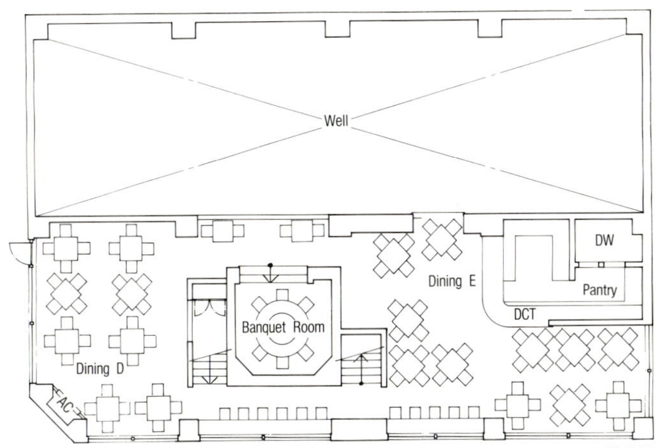

2F PLAN

工場街の個性的なビアマーケット

西院

京都府京都市右京区西院 リノ・ホテル地下１階

Beer Market SAI-IN

Saiin Ukyo-ku Kyoto, Designer Workshop Inc.

1

設計／ワークショップ
協力／設備　川口設備研究所　電気　山崎設備設計事務所　構造　プラスワン
施工／あめりか屋

1. 川面に張り出した客席のように宙に浮いたユカ席
View of the Yuka seatings from the banquet room

●揺らぐ水面の光と空間を満たす水音

オフィスや工場街という立地は，飲食業にとって必ずしも良い条件とはいえない。昼間はランチ需要しかないし，夜間は少し業態の間口を広げ，ニュアンスを変えねばならない場合が多い。京都の中心から外れた洛外の西院にできたこのビアレストランは，ホテルの地下にあり，周囲は大手企業の工場とその関連企業が多いという環境である。

このような立地のため，設計の意図は，グループ客などが多人数でも心地よく長居できる場を設定すること，同時にここにしかない場をつくり，空間のアイデンティティを明確にすることの二つが指向された。

京都を流れる鴨川の水面に張り出した仮設のお茶屋のように，奥のユカ席は鉄骨フレームによって宙に浮き，またユカ席わきの円形ガラステーブルには数個のスポットライトが集中し，水面に反射する光のように揺らぐ光がユカ席上部のテントに波紋を映し出す。さらに，このガラステーブルには水の循環する水盤が内部に仕掛けられ，音の高さがそれぞれに調節された水音が，音の和として空間を満たしている。

SAI-IN

Business and factory district are not always suitable for restaurants' location. Most people there eat out for lunches only, so restaurants often have to change their target customers and menus. This beer restaurant is in a basement of a hotel and the neighborhood includes a old big factory of a major manufacturer and its associated companies.

Considering the environment, a designer created a comfortable restaurant with unique character or identity for many guests, some are in groups, to stay there long.

Like a temporary restaurant room overlying on the Kamo River which runs through Kyoto, the back floor area is raised and supported by wood frames. A round showcase and table near the raised floor area is spotlighted by several lamps above and the reflection of wavy water is projected on the fabric tent hanging from the ceiling. The glass table has a water circulating flower bowl in it to make chordal sound filling the interior air.

2. 水音を響かせながらスポットの光を反射するファウンテン席のテーブル **Reflecting table top of the fountain seatings**

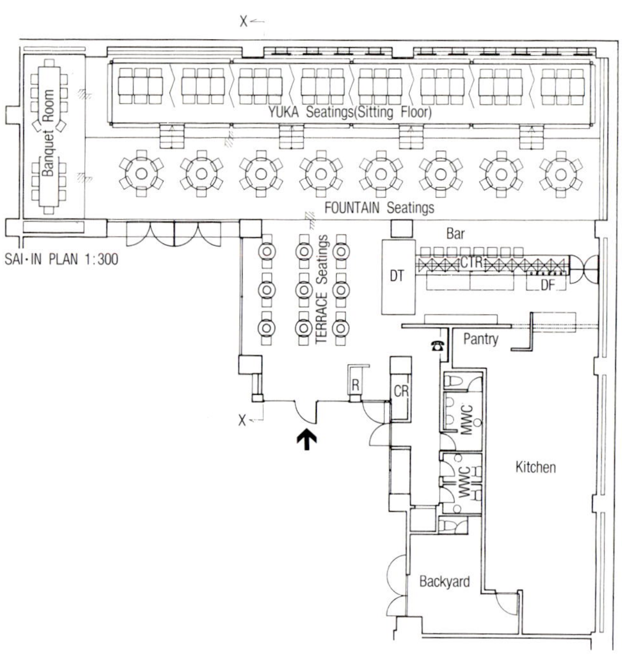

SAI・IN PLAN 1:300

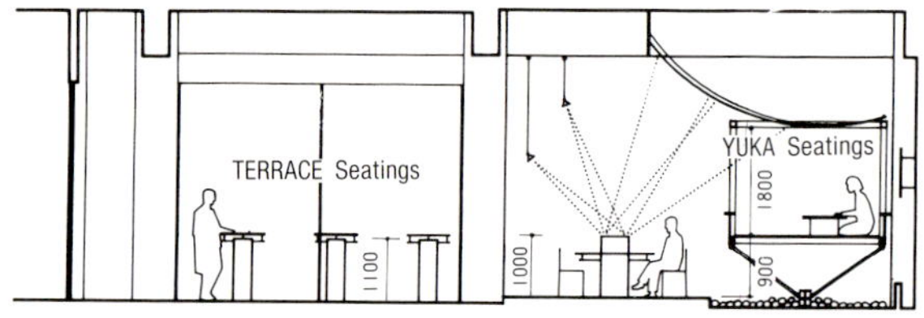

X-X SECTION 1:200

若いOLが集まる地下鉄駅内部のビアレストラン

キリンの館

大阪府大阪市都島区東野田町２丁目６－１ コムズガーデン地下１階

Beer Restaurant KIRIN-NO-YAKATA

Higashi-Noda-cho Miyakojima-ku Osaka
Designer Kenichiro Yamada

設計／K－７設計工房 山田健一郎 協力／陶器オブジェ 重松あゆみ
施工／乃村工芸社

1. 海底を歩く生物のメタファーとしての可動カウンタースツール
View of the counter stools from the dining A

1

2

●ステンレスの波が打ち寄せる海

地下鉄の駅は，階段で地上と結ばれた，人工照明による閉鎖的空間が多い。大阪の新しいビジネス街にできた地下鉄・京橋駅は，地上から掘り下げられたサンクンガーデンを持つ開放的空間が特徴であり，このビアレストランは自然光の入る中庭に面した地下１階レベルにある。

空間デザインは"波打ち際の海中"をテーマとしたもので，それもダイレクトな表現に訴えるのではなく，数枚のフィルターを掛けることによって客の空間に対するイメージが固定化するのを回避している。入り口をはじめ壁面に取り付けられた，陶芸アーチストの手になるオブジェはプランクトンをイメージしたものであり，カウンター席にあるキャスターの付いた椅子は海底を歩く生物であると同時に，想像上の動物であるキリンの化身でもある。しかし，それらは直接的に表現されることなく，来客に多様なイメージをもたらす知的プランクトンの一部として空間を漂うのである。

2. 入り口側から見た大テーブル席と客席C。壁から天井へと延びるステンレス製の波が海中を表す
View of the big table from the entry side

KIRIN-NO-YAKATA

With their cold artificial lighting, most subway stations look stifling and inhumane, accessed by just staircases.

Kyobashi subway station in a new office district of Osaka has a open space of a sunken garden. Facing the garden, this beer restaurant is situated in the same basement level as the station where people can enjoy natural light.

Designed upon a concept of "under sea waves", the interior used several screens to avoid common expression of the sea, not fixing visitors' impressions. Plankton-like objects by a ceramicist decorate the entrance walls. Caster chairs for a counter are like creatures (or kirin, imaginary animals) walking on the bottom of the sea. These chairs stimulate guests' imagination and they look drifting like planktons.

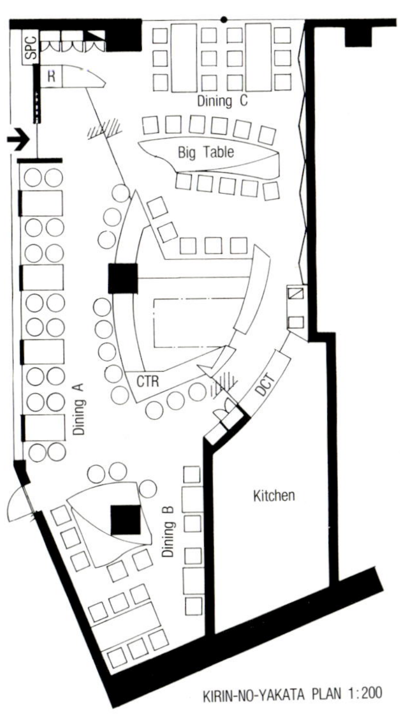

KIRIN-NO-YAKATA PLAN 1:200

“芭蕉の世界”がテーマの海鮮ビアレストラン

海鮮麦酒屋

大阪府大阪市中央区安土町3丁目2-14
河野本社ビル地下1階

Beer Inn & Bar
KAISEN BAKUSHUYA

Azuchi-cho Chuo-ku Osaka
Producer Fujio Maeyama

企画／目玉企画　前山富士雄
設計／クマ・クリエイト　野下達雄
施工／大丸装工事業部　藤原卓也

●様式から歴史性を取り去ったフォルム
建築デザインでポストモダニズムといえば，世界各国の歴史的な様式をその背景から切り離して引用し，コラージュする手法が一般に知られている。それは近代への反逆であり，クラシシズムへの回帰といえなくもない。大阪・安土町のビジネス街にできたこのレストランは，デザインのコンセプトをポストモダニズムよりさらに一歩進め，様式から歴史性を剝ぎとり，裸体のフォルムをさらすことにおいている。江戸時代の俳人・芭蕉の世界をテーマにしているものの，そこに表現されている和の世界はシンプルでありながら，ディテールは限りなくアーティスティックである。飛行船のように空中を浮遊する照明群は“ちょうちん”をイメージさせると同時に，アートとしてのインパクトを空間にもたらしている。
女性客をどのくらい集められるかがオフィス街の立地においては重要であるが，このアートを導入した空間は，海鮮料理の魅力もあいまって，若いOLを中心に幅広い客層で賑っている。

1. 中央客席Bの天井を浮遊する照明オブジェ群
The lighting objects of the dining B

KAISEN BAKUSHUYA
Collages, quotations of various styles from different periods and mix of various cultural concepts are common method of post-modern architecture.
It might rise revolt against our age or revolt to classicism. This restaurant opened in a business area of Azuchi-machi town in Osaka went far beyond a way of post-modernism and wiped off the Zeitgeist from the style to expose naked forms.
The design concept was expressing images of a world of Matsuo Basho, an eminent haiku poet in Edo era. The design was simple and harmonious, and details were marvelously artistic. Lamps were like air-ships, reminiscent of Japanese lanterns, accentuating the interior.
Project location is very important to attract female customers in this type of business area and in that sense this sea food restaurant is a hit, visited by a variety of many customers, above all, young working girls.

1

2

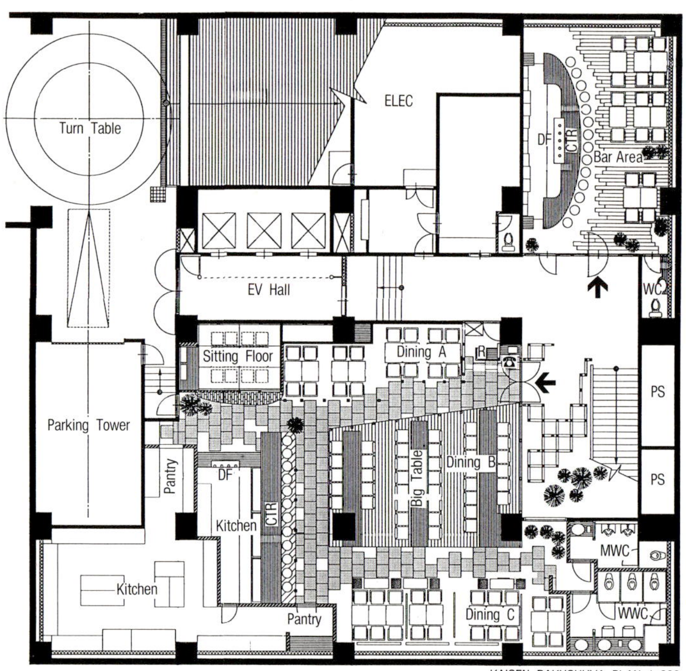

KAISEN BAKUSHUYA PLAN 1:300

2. 天井から自然石を吊り下げたバーコーナー
The hanging stones of the bar area

柔らかさに包まれたカジュアル・ダイニングバー

ポーミエ 渋谷店

東京都渋谷区東1丁目26-20 東京建物東渋谷ビル1・2階

設計／建築 カジマデザイン 栗原成美 藤 教生
内装 カジマデザイン 奥村 修 神村真由美
施工／建築 鹿島建設・西松建設・東急建設共同企業体
内装 ウィング・インテリア

Café 1ér

Higashi Shibuya-ku Tokyo, Designer Kajima Corporation

1. 布の吊り下げられた階段吹き抜けを2階より見る
View of the stairwell from the second floor

1

●時代によって古びないデザイン
デザインは時代とともに変わっていき，今日，新しいものは数年後には古びてしまう。しかし，人の心を本質的にとらえ，受け継がれてきた空間は，過去に何度も見た記憶があるため最先端のデザインという印象を与えないが，古びることもない。
東京・並木橋にできたこのダイニングバーは，いつの時代にも変わらない人の心と手が創り出した温かな感覚と，トータルにバランスの取れたコンテンポラリーな雰囲気をコンセプトに企画された。道路から見ると宝石箱のように優しい光を街並みにこぼす内部空間は，布が効果的に柔らかさを演出し，また手づくりに近い形で作られたオリジナルの家具やアイアンワークが，表情豊かな素材感，色，形によって強い存在感を放っている。
これらのエレメントは既存の建築部材とぶつかり合い，ミックスされて独特の表情を生みだし，ここを訪れるビジネスマンやOLを夜毎楽しませる。

2. 奥客席Bより2階客席A方向を見る
2F：View of the dining A

2

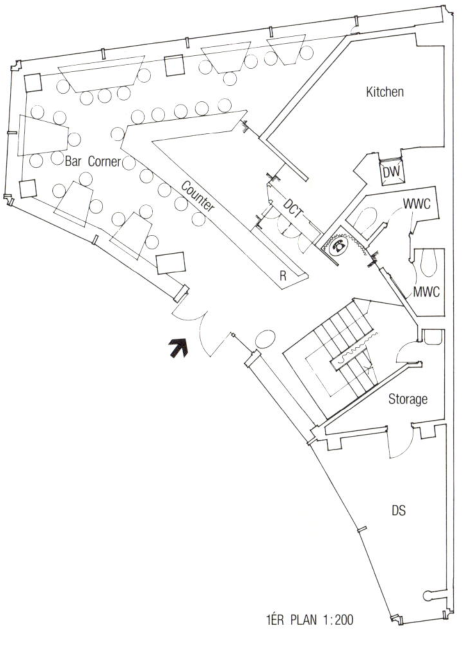

1 ÉR

Design changes with the time and period. Today's new design will become out of fashion in several years. If one interior design captures people's mind deeply, and it will last long and will not be easily become "out", as it appealed to our deja-vu memory, instead of giving an "in " impression.

This dining bar in Namikibashi, Tokyo was designed to have a look of hand-made touch and everlasting humane warmth in well-balanced contemporary sense. Seen from the outside, it appears to be a jewelry box radiating a soft light. With effectively used fabrics, the interior touches you gently. Custom made furniture and iron work are telling stories of themselves. Expressive materials, texture, colors and forms are unique. The originally designed elements are mixed with ready made materials and fused to make special expressions to please night guests — business men and women.

1

チェーン店の殻を打ち破ったデザインの居酒屋

つぼ八 ペンギンズ・スクエア店

大阪府大阪市北区堂山町6-5 ペンギンズ・スクエア地下1・2階

Casual Restaurant TSUBOHACHI

Doyama-cho Kita-ku Osaka, Designer Hiroji Yoshio

設計／インテリアデザインオフィスノブ 吉尾浩次
施工／イトイ大建

1. 中地下1階の座敷席内部
MB1F: View of the sitting floor
2. 二層分を貫く自立した壁を地下2階客席Gより見る
B1F: View of the dining E from the dining G 2

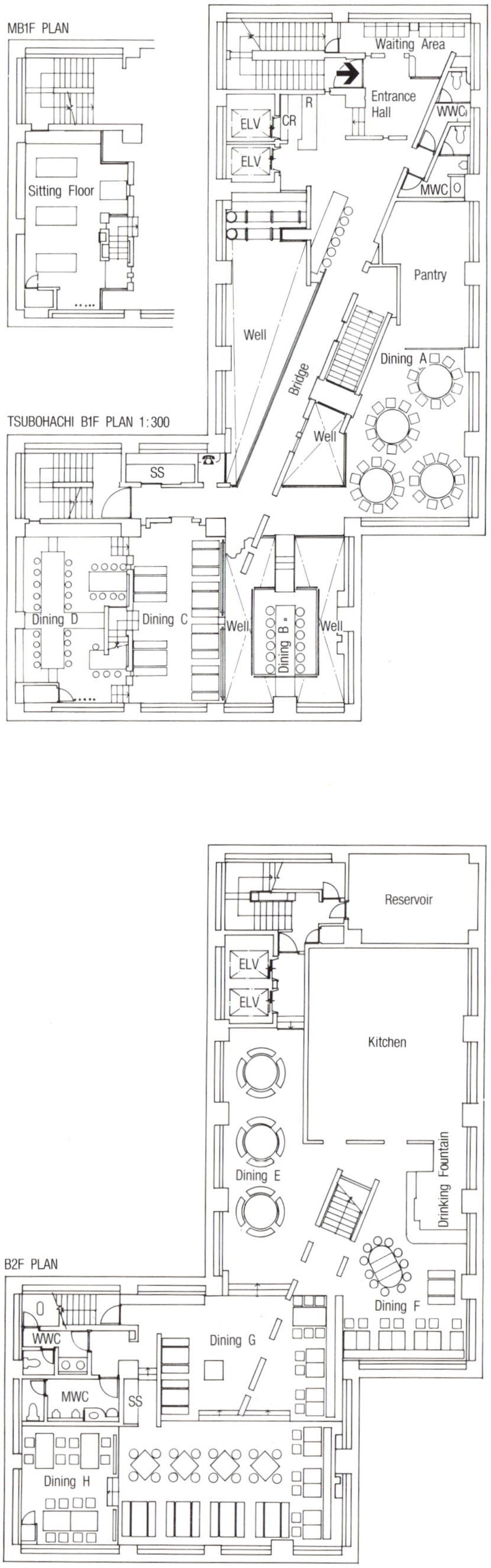

3

●自立する壁が生み出す多様な空間シーン
均一な味，サービス，デザインを武器にレストランチェーンは発展してきた。しかし，それらの特徴は均一さゆえに飽きられ，特に競合店の多い激戦地域では勝ち抜く要因とならないことも，しばしばである。
大阪・キタの繁華街にできたこの居酒屋レストランはチェーン店であるが，内部デザインは独自の展開をしている。計画にあたって要望されたのは，入り口は小さく，店内の様子を見えにくくすること，天井高のある大空間を生かしつつも一目で全体が見渡せないこと，デザインによる差異化を図り，来客の記憶に残るシーンを演出できることなどであった。
これらの条件をクリアするために造り出されたのが，地下2階から地下1階へと突き抜けた巨大な自立する壁である。店内を斜めに貫通する長短3枚の壁は，地下2階レベルでは客席を細かいコーナーに分割し，また地下1階レベルではブリッジとなって客席へのアプローチ機能を果たしている。

3. 吹き抜けに浮かぶ地下1階客席B
B1F: View of the dining B and well

TUBOHACHI Penguin's Square
Chain restaurants have been developed by their standardized food, service, interior design. However, some people are now fed up with such uniform style, so many chain restaurants in competitive areas have to endeavor to survive.
This chain Japanese bar and restaurant opened in Kita, downtown of Osaka is exceptional in its independent interior design. The project requirements: making small entrance to prevent passers-by from looking into the interior, making the most of high ceiling and wide site, creating some elements for guests not to look over the interior and giving a memorable impression to visitors by the interior. To fulfill these conditions, a designer created one bulky wall (with sub walls) penetrating the space diagonally from the first to the second basement. Also, these walls divide areas and functions as a bridge (or approach) on the first basement level.

1

茶道の美学をメタルで表現したステーキ店

ピアクリスタル

兵庫県神戸市中央区東川崎町１丁目8-1　オーガスタプラザ17階

Steak Restaurant PIER CRYSTAL

Higashikawasaki-cho Chuo-ku Kobe, Designer Kan Izue Architects & Associates

設計／ 出江建築事務所
施工／大和建設　園田本店(金属工事)

1. ビルの公共通路から見た入り口まわり
View of the entry from the public passage
2. ステーキ・神戸亭の窓側に面した客席
Steak counters of the Kobetei

3

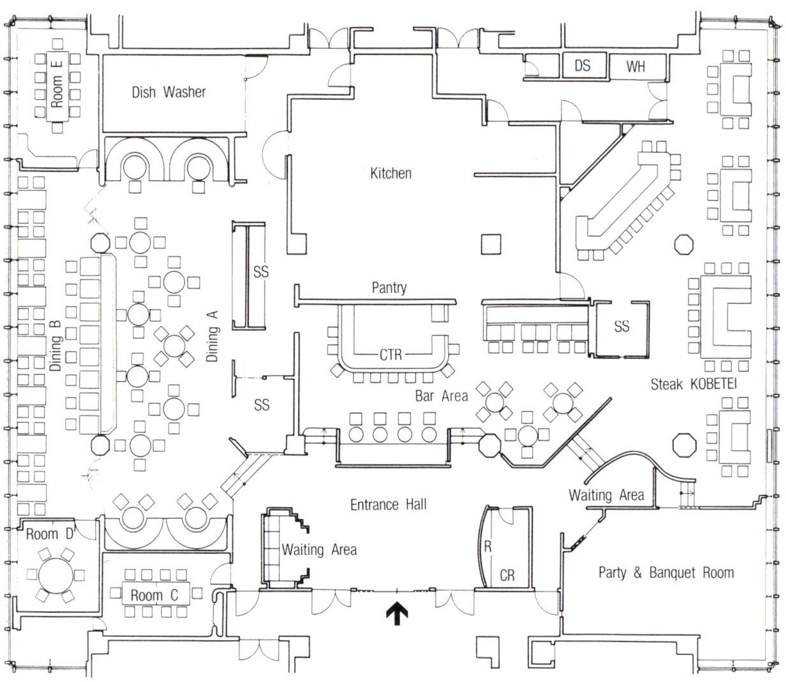

PIER CRYSTAL PLAN 1:300

●古びる美をメタルで表現

数寄屋造りとは，草庵茶室に代表されるように自然の素材の美を取り入れ，装飾を排除した精神で創られたものであった。しかし，時代が経ち，様式として定着すると，当初の精神は忘れ去られ，形式のみが独り歩きするようになる。

神戸のウオーターフロントにできたこのレストランは，数寄屋の当初の精神に立ち戻り，工業製品としてありふれた存在であるメタルを使って，素材が古びていくなかに美を創出しようという意図でデザインされた。古びるとは，単に物が古くなるという意味ではなく，古くなるほど美しくなるという意味であり，これは日本に古くからあ

4

る茶の精神を背景にした"侘びる""さびる"という美学に深く通じるものである。
ここで使われている金属は，やがて酸化して表面的なてらてらした輝きがなくなり，全体に古色蒼然となって，ある種の精神性を孕んでストイックな表情になる。"古美る"とは素材や形の表面的なものではなく，精神性の中から生まれるものなのである。

3. 入り口右側に配されたパーティー＆宴会室内部
View of the party and banquet room
4. 店内中央のバーコーナーを神戸亭側より見る
View of the bar area from the Kobetei

PIER CRYSTAL
Sukiya is a Japanese traditional architectural style exemplified by Soan-chashitu, a small tea ceremony room, using beauty of natural material and minimizing decorative elements. However, the style changed as times goes by and the original idea was often ignored, and finally only the superficial form was respected and used now in most cases.
This restaurant in a Kobe waterfront area used this Sukiya style, considering its original spirit and useing interestingly industrial materials to show the beauty of of a rusting process. Aging in this country do not mean just becoming old physically but a turning beautiful through time both for the man and art. It is closely related to Japanese traditional aesthetic of "wabi" and "sabi", having common ground of Zen philosophy.
Metallic materials used here will be rusted and lose shiny texture of the surfaces but they would finally appear to express stoic beauty. Aging is not a superficial materialistic process but a spiritual change.

公園に面したホテル内のステーキ&シーフードレストラン

アルテミス

大阪府大阪市西区靱本町2丁目2-20 ホテルアルパ大阪地下1階

Seafood & Steak Restaurant ARTEMIS

Utsubo-honmachi Nishi-ku Osaka, Designer Kazuhiro Motomochi

●柔らかく包み込む月の女神・アルテミスの光
シティホテルには，そのグレードにふさわしい飲食施設が必ず含まれている。それらは，ホテルに宿泊している客だけでなく，外部からやってくる客を対象にしている場合も多い。大阪には珍しく緑の豊かな公園に面したホテルの地下１階にできたこのレストランは，外部の社用接待客とファミリー客を対象としたステーキコーナーと，若い女性がメーンのシーフードコーナーの二つに分かれている。
ギリシャをテーマとしたホテルにふさわしく，月の女神・アルテミスを店名にした空間は，光がデザインのモチーフである。店内を二つに分ける柱型の上部には，女神の衣服をイメージさせるFRP製のドレープが取り付けられ，内蔵した照明により柔らかい光を放つ。また，柱型に沿って床の上に置かれた光のパーティションは綿布製で，影のない影を浮かび上がらせる。この二つの光は，ステーキカウンター上部のステンレスフードに映り込み，その増幅された照明効果が空間を柔らかく包み込んで，月の女神・アルテミスの光を演出する。

ARTEMIS
City hotels have either restaurants or eateries suitable for their scale and grade. The restaurants are used not only hotel guests but also visitors.
This restaurant opened in a basement of a hotel surrounded by rich plants, unusually in Osaka, was planed to provide steaks for business people and sea food for young women.
As the hotel was designed upon an image of the Greek myth, this restaurant used a leitmotif of Artemis, the goddess of the moon and adopted a effective lighting for the design concept. Above columns, dividing the interior into two, fiber reinforced plastic drapes were installed as an image of the robe of the goddess and the built-in lamps give off dim and mild light.
Along with columns, canvas lighting partitions project vague shadows here and there. A stainless roof above a steak cocking counter reflected these lights and shadows marvelously. The whole interior space is, so to speak, filled with the soft light of Artemis.

設計／東畑建築事務所　本持一博
協力／特殊照明　ライズ　岡幸男　家具　高島屋装飾部
施工／不二建設　大丸装工事業部

1. ステーキコーナーとシーフードコーナーを分ける照明オブジェ群
View of the lighting objects from the steak area

2

2. ステーキカウンターとミラー貼りの排気フード **View of the steak counter and exhaust hood**

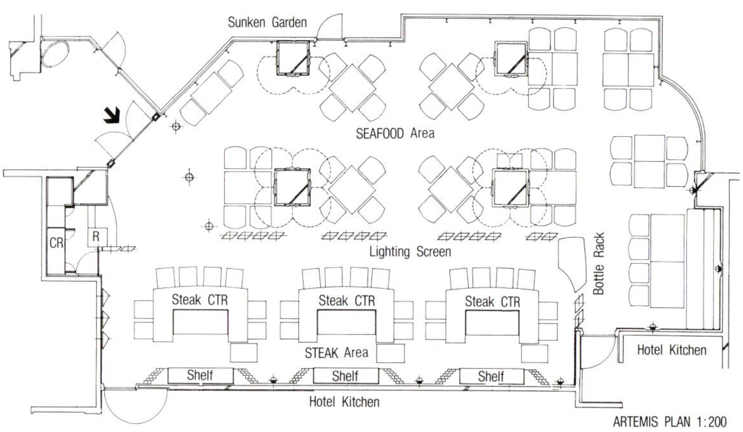

ARTEMIS PLAN 1:200

三次曲線による力強い外観のステーキレストラン

ジロー

福岡県久留米市合川町608-1

Steak Restaurant JIRO

Aikawa-cho Kurume-shi Fukuoka

Designer Toshiharu Nakayama

設計／ナカヤマ・トシ設計　トシ・アソシエイツ　中山俊治

施工／丸山建設

1. 東側外観全景。屋根はステンレスシート葺き

View of the east side from a rice field

1

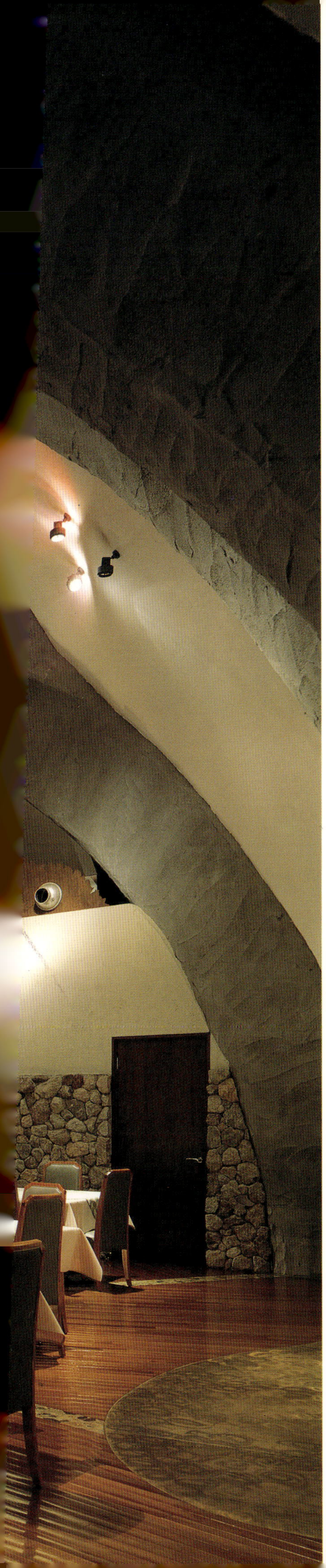

2

●大地の熱とダイナミックさ

高速道路の発達によって日本中に道路網が張り巡らされるようになり，ロードサイド型の店舗も増加の一途をたどっている。特に自動車専用道路のインターチェンジから市街地へ至る地域は，レストランやカーショールームが立ち並ぶ，競争の激しい立地となっている。

九州・久留米市の郊外にできたこのレストランは，インターチェンジから市内へ至る道路に面しているが，周囲のありふれた外観の店舗とは違った，個性的で，しかも力強さと安定感を表すデザインが志向された。3次曲線で構成された巨大な柱と梁は鉄骨造で，特殊な樹脂モルタルで塗り込められ，また，内外の壁面には地球のマントルが溶けて流れ出てできた火山岩を使用し，建物に大地の熱とダイナミックさを表現している。

この建築をデザインするに際しては，イメージを具体化したパースと模型を繰り返し作っては，やり直し，最後に図面を起こすという時間と手間のかかる方法が取られた。

2. 厨房側より入り口方向を見た客席全景
View of the dining hall from the kitchen

JIRO

With the development of network of highways in Japan, so-called roadside shops and restaurants increased. Areas near interchanges and towards towns or cities are competitive commercial sites particularly for restaurants and car showrooms.

Facing a road from an interchange to the center of the city, this restaurants and car showroooms in a suburb of Kurume city in Kyushu island had to be designed uniquely and to show a sense of stability, easily distinguishable from neighboring ordinary shops and restaurants. In this project, big steel columns and beams, mortar, and volcanic rock from a mantle are used for both exterior and interior walls to express the heat and dynamism of the earth.

The designer spent a lot of time in making models and sketching or perspective drawings again and again to get the final presentation work.

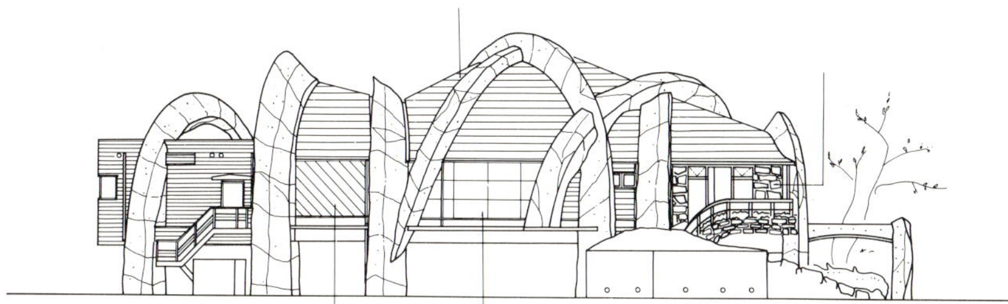

SOUTH ELEVATION 1:400

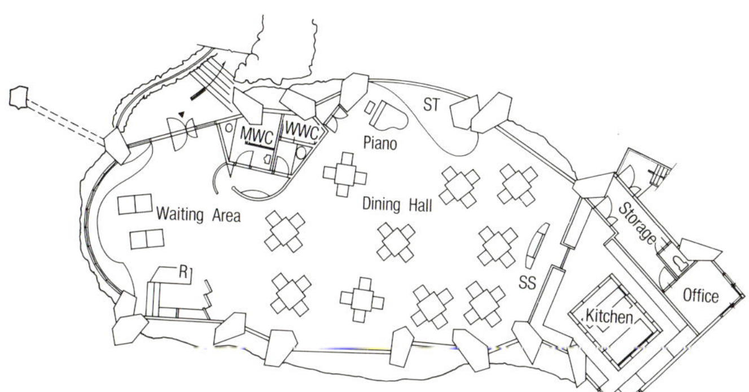

2F PLAN

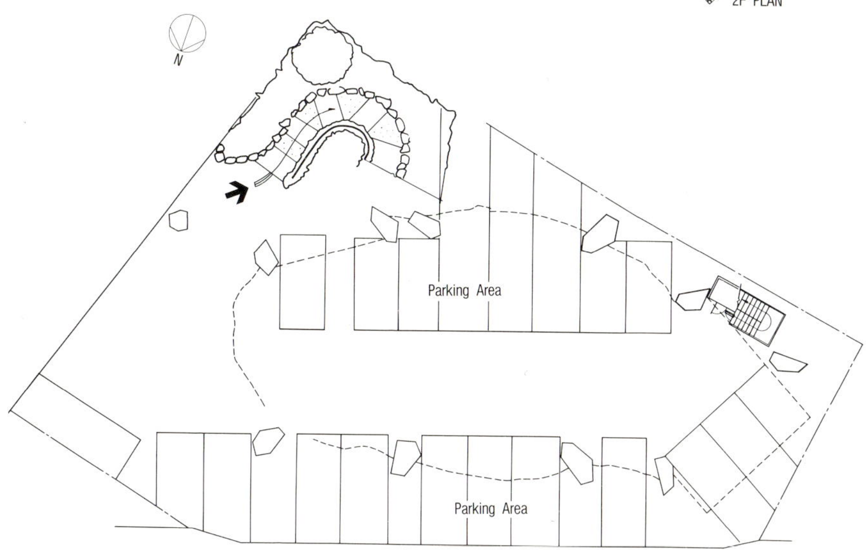

JIRO 1F PLAN 1:400

1

古材により風格と年輪を創出したステーキ会席店

いわい

東京都町田市原町田4丁目7-4 リンスワンビル地下１階

Steak Restaurant IWAI

Haramachida Machida-shi Tokyo, Designer Sumio Ishikawa

設計／マカンボ建築設計事務所
石川純夫　斎藤正美　島　淳子
施工／小池工務店

1. 古レンガ積みの風除室を入り口から見る
View of the windbreak room from the entry
2. 中央通路からステーキカウンター席と入り口方向を見る
View of the corridor from the kitchen side

2

3

●日本と西洋の古材を混交して使う
古い民家で使われていた柱や梁などの材木，および，使い古したレンガを使って店舗を造ることは，資源を大事にするというだけでなく，新しくできた店舗が，それらの古材を使うことによって以前の歴史を思い起こさせ，歳月を経た年輪を持つことを可能とする。
東京のベッドタウン・町田市にできたこのレストランは，昼間はフランス料理のコースメニュー，夜間は会席料理とステーキのコースメニューをメーンとしており，この地域としてはハイグレードなクラスに属する。
内部に使われている40本以上の柱と，それを上廻る数の梁は古い日本の民家で使われていたケヤキ材であり，また，壁面の大部分を構成するレンガも使い古された洋館のものである。さらに，窓に嵌め込まれたアンティークのステンドグラスやエッチンググラス，しっくい壁などが，ゆったりと食事のできる空間に西洋と日本の入りまじった独特の雰囲気を醸し出している。

3. ステーキカウンター席内部を通路から見る
View of the steak counter from the entry

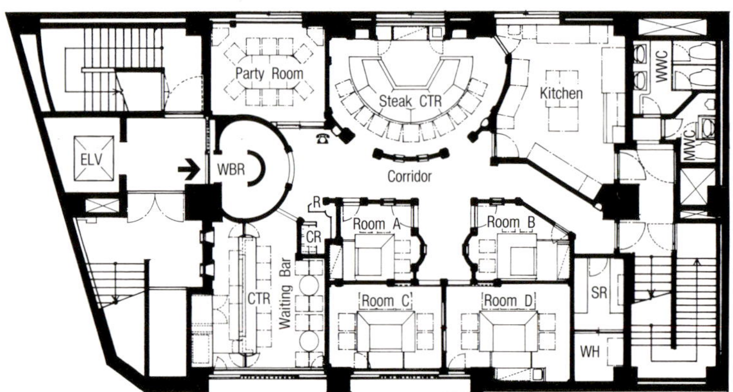

IWAI PLAN 1:250

IWAI
Using salvage materials such as columns, beams, and bricks from old houses is useful and effective in terms of recycling, and it makes it possible for designers to give new projects old or antique look effect, which can let people remember old memory.
This restaurant in Machida city, a bed room town of Tokyo, offers courses of French cuisine in day time and at night Japanese kaiseki zen style food and steak courses. Considering the project location and neighborhood, this restaurant can be qualified as a high grade one.
More than forty old zelkova columns and beams were taken from old Japanese houses. Bricks used for most walls were from an old Western house. Antique stained glass of windows, etched glass, and plaster walls create an intriguing atmosphere for dining area, mixing Western and Japanese architectural elements.

ステーキとしゃぶしゃぶをメーンとした郊外型レストラン

オクスン 北方

岐阜県本巣郡北方小柳932

Steak & Shabu-Shabu Restaurant OXEN Kitagata

Kitagata-cho Motosu-gun Gifu, Designer Shigeru Nishibe

設計／ニシベデザイン事務所　西部　茂
協力／山崎建築事務所　山崎規正
施工／苅谷建設

1. 南側正面外観をパーキングエリアより見る
View of the south side from the parking area

1

●ハードな素材による和らいだ空間
ステーキ料理は西洋から伝わってきたものであり，しゃぶしゃぶ料理の源流は中国にある。ともに肉を主体とした料理だが，今や日本人の味覚になじみ，ポピュラーな存在となっている。名古屋から鉄道で約１時間の岐阜市は昔から繊維や衣料の生産地として栄えてきた都市であるが，このステーキとしゃぶしゃぶを提供するレストランは岐阜市から車で約10分の場所にできた。
車で来る客を意識してデザインされたモダンで目立つ外観は，アクセントカラーとしてインパクトの強い赤を使っているが，逆に内部は日本的な意匠を巧みに使っているのが空間上の特徴である。光庭または坪庭は京都の町家でよく見られるデザインで，小さなスペースにより内部空間に自然を感じさせるための手法であるが，この店では客席を二つに分割するためのクッションとして使用されている。また，壁はモルタル掻き落としとなっているが，この仕上げは日本古来の土壁をイメージさせ，客に親しみ易さを与えている。

2. 入り口側から見たメーンダイニング客席
View of the main dining from the entry
3. 店内を左右に分割する中央の光り庭
View of the courtyard from the cashier

OXEN
Steaks originally came from the West and Shabu-shabu style, boiled beef cocking, might be from China. In the long both foods became very popular and familiar to Japanese people. Gifu city, about one hour trip by train from Nagoya has been prosperous by producing textiles and clothing. Some ten minutes' drive from Gifu city takes you to this restaurant of steaks and shabu-shabu. The outstandingly modern exterior was designed for drivers and the red is used as a strong impact. The interior, however, is tactically designed with Japanese elements. Hikari-niwa or tsubo-niwa (a small garden) is often seen in a traditional Kyoto style house for people to feel the nature, and in this restaurant hikari-niwa was introduced to divide two dining areas just like a sort of small buffer zone. Walls are scratched mortar whose finish reminds us of a traditional soil walls familiar to visitors.

3

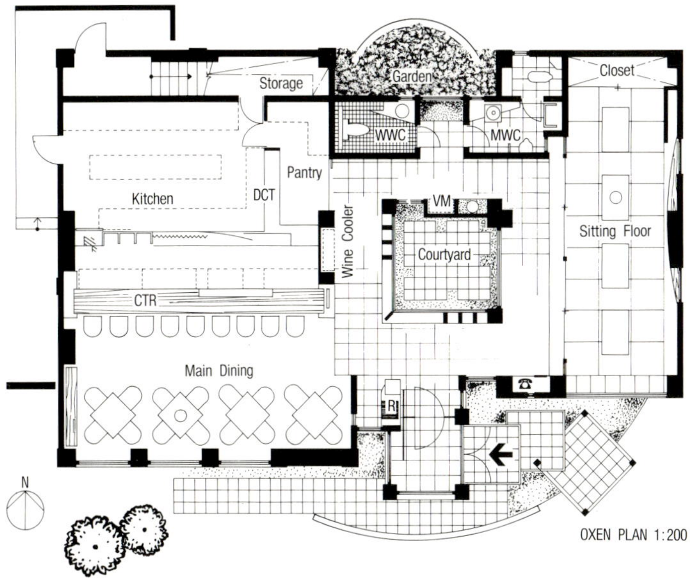

OXEN PLAN 1:200

2

美味な肉を安く提供するステーキ割烹

楽亭

東京都墨田区吾妻橋２丁目２－４ フェスティ・ワン３階

Steak Restaurant RAKUTEI

Azumabashi Sumida-ku Tokyo, Designer Yoshihiko Ishihara

設計／遊アソシエイツ　石原嘉彦　旭 統志
施工／布谷

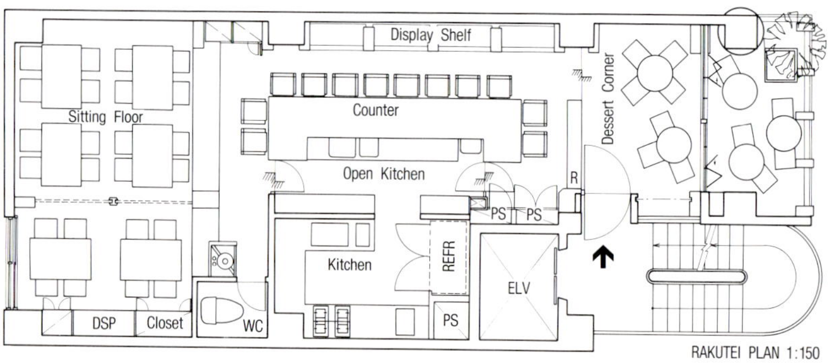

RAKUTEI PLAN 1:150

1

●花火をテーマとした空間デザイン

日本ではステーキは高級料理である。戦後の貧しかった時代はさておき，近年になっても国内の牧畜農家を保護するために安い牛肉の輸入をストップしてきたためであろう。東京の下町・浅草にできたこのレストランは，肉屋さんが安くて美味な牛肉を直接，消費者に提供しようという目的で企画された。ここで提供されるのは山形牛とよばれる最高級の牛肉で，メニューはステーキとしゃぶしゃぶ料理がメーンである。

新築された自社ビルの３階に位置する店内は，毎年この地域で開催される隅田川の花火にちなんだ"銀河花火"がテーマであり，デザートスペースの"青炎"という

2

題のつけられた壁画や，カウンター上部の波打つ吊り天井も，このテーマに沿ったものである。奥の座敷席にある赤く塗られた格天井からの赤い光と，壁面パネルの意匠も下町情緒を感じさせるものであり，器を展示してある飾り棚の大谷石が日本的空間に重厚で落ち着いた雰囲気を与えている。

1. 奥の小上がり席と間接照明を持つ飾り棚
   View of the sitting floor
2. 小上がり席側から見たカウンター席
   View of the counter from the sitting floor

RAKUTEI

In Japan a steak used to be a rich food. Even today some kind of steak are expensive and luxurious, for the Japanese government banned to import low price foreign beef to protect domestic stock breeders.

To provide low price and good beef with customers directly, this restaurant in a downtown of Akasakusa, Tokyo was planed. In this restaurant, Yamagata beef, one of high grade Japanese beefs are served as steaks or shabu-shabu. Located on the third floor of a newly built owner's building, the project was designed, expressing a concept of "galaxy of fire works", as the restaurant is near the Sumida river, where people enjoy seeing a festival of fire work show every summer. In this project, walls of an area for serving dessert are decorated by painting titled "Blue Flame".

Also waving suspended ceiling above a counter echoes to the concept. Red lattice ceiling above tatami mat seating area was designed to represent traditional downtown people's (downtown Tokyoites') mind. A Oya-ishi, a kind of tuff-made decorative shelves for displaying pottery gives static feeling to the Japanese style interior.

角閃石の石鍋で料理する石焼き・しゃぶしゃぶ料理店

石土炉（いしどろ）

東京都千代田区神田駿河台2丁目1-17 ジローお茶の水本館5階

Steak & Shabu-Shabu Restaurant ISHIDORO

Kanda-surugadai Chiyoda-ku Tokyo, Designer Masanobu Hasegawa

設計／長谷川正允建築事務所
施工／建築　大末建設　内装　匠工業

1. 店内中央客席Aの待合側より奥の飾り棚方向を見る
View of the dining A from the waiting area side

1

2

●アジアと西洋の香りが混交した空間

通常，ステーキは鉄板で調理したり，しゃぶしゃぶは胴鍋を利用するのが一般的である。ところが東京・お茶の水にできたこのレストランは，石鍋を使って両方の料理を調理するのが特徴であり，売り物となっている。もともと，石鍋を使った調理方法は韓国にあり，店名も韓国・済州島のイシドール牧場から採られたものである。

空間デザインも韓国の古い民家の記憶などが採り入れられているが，それだけではなく，南スペインなど南欧の国の香りもミックスされている。この二つのモチーフに共通しているのは，訪れる者を迎える空間の落ち着きと温かさ，ゆったりと流れる時間，心地よい静けさであり，それを具現化するために様々な素材が使われた。

ウォームグレーの石貼りの床と白い漆喰壁，生地のままの太い木の柱や飾り棚や造作類，そして石洞窟のような化粧室といった各部のデザインがコンセプトを実体化し，西洋とアジアの香りの入りまじったホスピタリティあふれる空間を創出している。

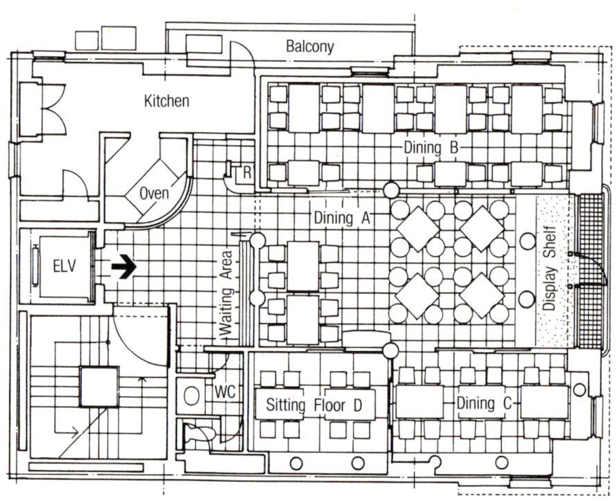

ISHIDORO PLAN 1:200

2. 座敷席D内部を客席Aより見る
Interior view of the sitting floor D

ISHIDORO

Steaks are cocked on steel pans or plates and shabu-shabu (boiled beef) are with copper shabu-shabu pans. However, in this restaurant opened in Ochanomizu, Tokyo characteristically uses stone pans for both steaks and shabu-shabu. Stone pans has been used in Korea and the restaurant was named after Isidoro ranch in Cheju do of the South Korea.

The interior uses design elements from Korean old house, mixed with those from southern Europe (particularly south Spain). These three motifs have in common, relaxation and warmth to guests, slow pace of life cycle, and comfortable quietness, which all are embodied in various materials.

Fit to the concept, warm gray stone floor, white plaster walls, unvarnished wood columns and decorative shelves, cave-like washrooms, and other details represent hospitality in both Eastern and Western ways.

CAFE RESTAURANTS & FASTFOOD RESTAURANTS

大樹のイメージが４層を貫くカフェ・レストラン

ゼクウ

東京都中央区銀座３丁目２-11

Café Restaurant ZEQUE

Ginza Chuo-ku Tokyo
Designer Kazuhiro Nishino

設計／西野和宏
施工／セブン工芸

1. 鍛鉄の樹木に囲まれた1階入り口まわりを道路側より見る
Night view of the entry from the street
2. 地下1階のバーフロアをパントリー側より見る。
大樹の根がデザインのモチーフとなっている
B1F: View of the bar floor from the pantry side

1

●一本の大樹をストーリーにした手作り空間
一つの空間が物語性を持ったデザインで展開されることは多い。しかし，地下１階から地上３階までの４層の空間が，一つの物語を物理的に表現した例は少ないだろう。
デザインのテーマは，ファサードを覆う鍛鉄製の幹と葉が表しているように樹木である。それも小さな木ではなく，４階の高さにまで達する大樹である。内部空間は地中にあたる地下１階が大樹の根と水と砂を，地表にあたる１階が葉の生い茂る木陰を，２階が枝の内部を，そして３階が樹上の空をモチーフとしている。それぞれの空間は木材を基本に，鉄，石，ステンドグラスなどの

2

工芸作家により手作りで制作され，それぞれが互いに調和しながら，独自の世界を創り出している。
東京・銀座にできたこのカフェレストランは改装に際して，店名も現在のように変えられたが，地域にこのような手作りの温か味のある店舗が珍しいこともあって，若い女性やOLの注目するところとなり，ちょっと気になる存在として話題になっている。

ZEQUE
Designing space is somewhat similar to telling stories. It can be said that this project is depended upon a story-telling design. It would be rare that whole project was designed by one story concept from its basement to the fifth floor.
A tree is the main theme of this interior design, as you see it in iron trunk and foliage covering the facade. The tree was big.
The basement is designed as underground world for roots and water. The first floor is thicket, the second is inside of trunk, the third is sky above the tree. Each floor is designed by craftsmen of stone work, iron work, stained glass, etc. to represent each concept. Harmonized and unified, the total project expresses a world of a tree.
This cafe and restaurant in Ginza, Tokyo, originally had a different name and it was changed when renovated. Warm, unique and decorative, this project looks outstanding. Today as a trendy place, the intriguing design attracts young women and working girls.

3

3. 空をモチーフにした3階パーティールームの照明
3F : View of the party room from the entry side
4. 大樹の木陰を表現した1階客席を待合側から見る
1F : View of the dining B from the waiting area

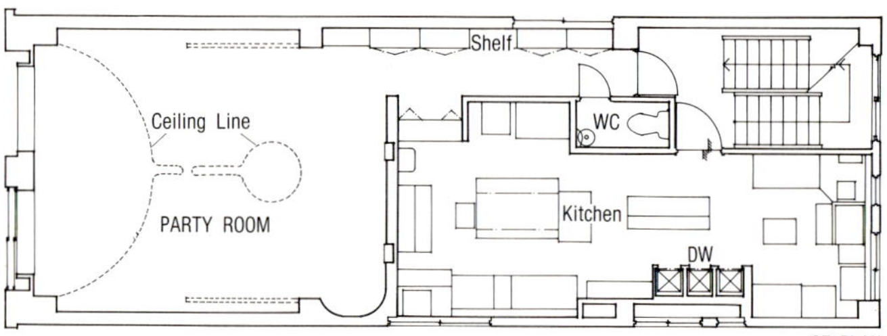

3F PLAN

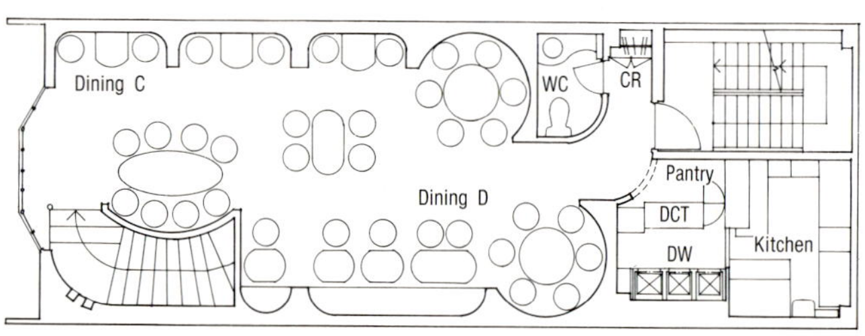

2F PLAN

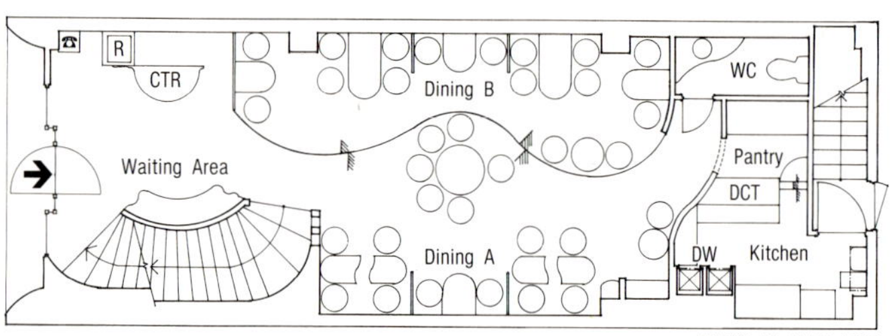

ZEQUE 1F PLAN 1:200

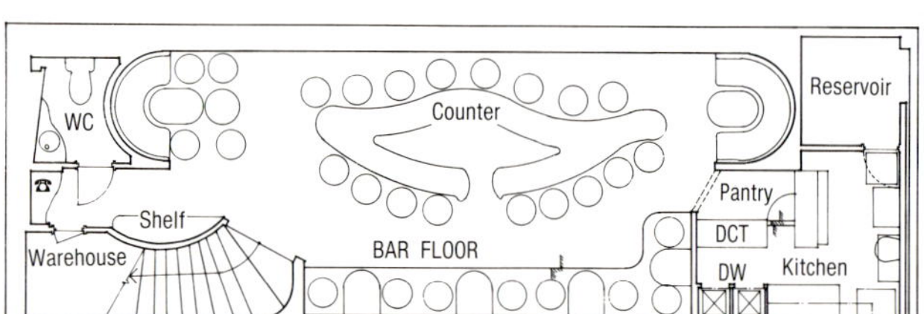

B1F PLAN

4

1

インドの香りのするカフェ&ダイニングバー

オリエンタルウェーブ&ラジーニ

東京都新宿区新宿５丁目17-13　東京大飯店ビル１・２階

Café ORIENTAL WAVE & Dining Bar RAJINI

Shinjuku Shinjuku-ku Tokyo
Designer Koichi Yasunaga

設計／鹿島　イリア　安永孝一　島村こみち　粕川愛子
施工／鹿島　イリア

1. 靖国通りに面した入り口まわり外観夜景　Night view of the entry from the street
2. 入り口側から見た1階カフェ客席全景　1F: View of the interior from the entry

●コロニアルスタイルがベース

東京・新宿にある東京大飯店は古い歴史を持つ有名な中国レストランであるが，時代の流れを反映し，若い女性にも好まれるように順次リニューアルする計画がたてられた。その第一弾として９階建てのビルの１・２階がカフェとダイニングバーへと改装され，東京大飯店の新しい顔としてのイメージをアピールしている。目立つように２階までの高さとされたファサード，および内部空間はコロニアルスタイルをベースにしており，中国料理からインド，アジア料理などへメニュー内容を広げたことに対応したデザインとなっている。１階のカフェは白い格子とバーズアイメープルの円柱で構成され，床がベージュ系の大理石と木のパターン貼りによるコロニアルスタイルとされ，椅子の張り地には翡翠のイメージを表すグリーンが用いられた。また，生のピアノ演奏を楽しみながら食事のできる２階のダイニングバーは，１階と同じくコロニアルスタイルをベースにしながらも，アートワークや屏風，花器などで変化をつけた空間となっている。

2

ORIENTAL WAVE & RAJINI

Tokyo Daihanten, an old famous Chinese restaurant in Shinjuku, Tokyo was renovated to catch up contemporary design trend and to attract young female guests. The first step of the renovation project was done for the first and the second floor of the nine-story building to show a new face of the restaurant.

The facade was the second story level high to stand out and the interior was designed mostly upon a concept of colonial style. The menu was changed to include Indian and other Asian foods.

A cafe on the first floor had white lattices and birds eye maple columns, beige marble floor, patterned wood work, and furniture with jade-like green plates.

A dining bar on the second floor was also designed by colonial style, accentuated by pieces of art work : folding screens, vases, etc. Here guests enjoy dining, hearing live piano music.

4

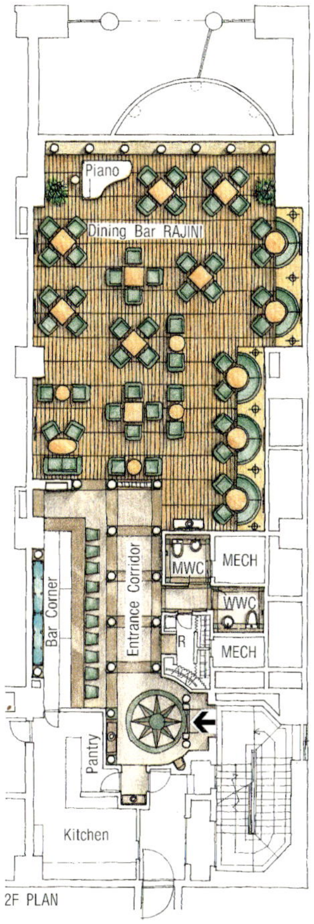

2F PLAN

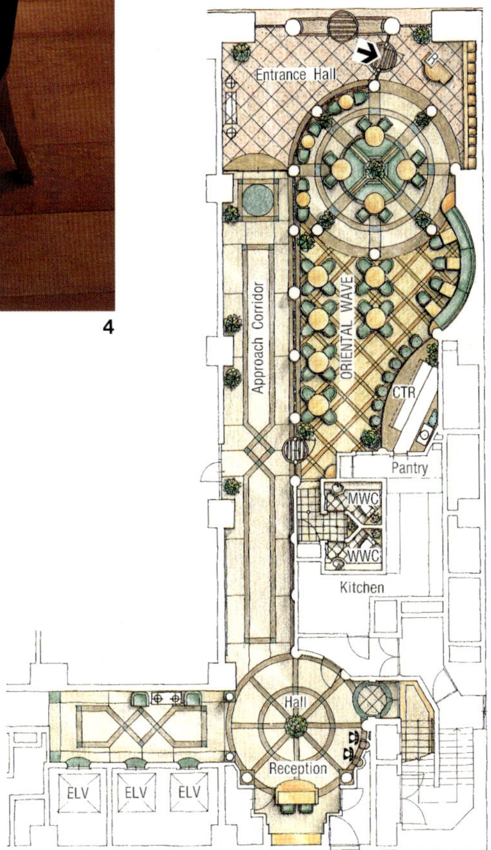

ORIENTAL WAVE & RAJINI 1F PLAN 1:300

3. 入り口通路を通して2階ダイニングバー客席方向を見る
2F : View of the entrance corridor from the entry
4. ピアノ生演奏を楽しめる2階ダイニングバーの客席
2F : View of the seatings from the piano side

3

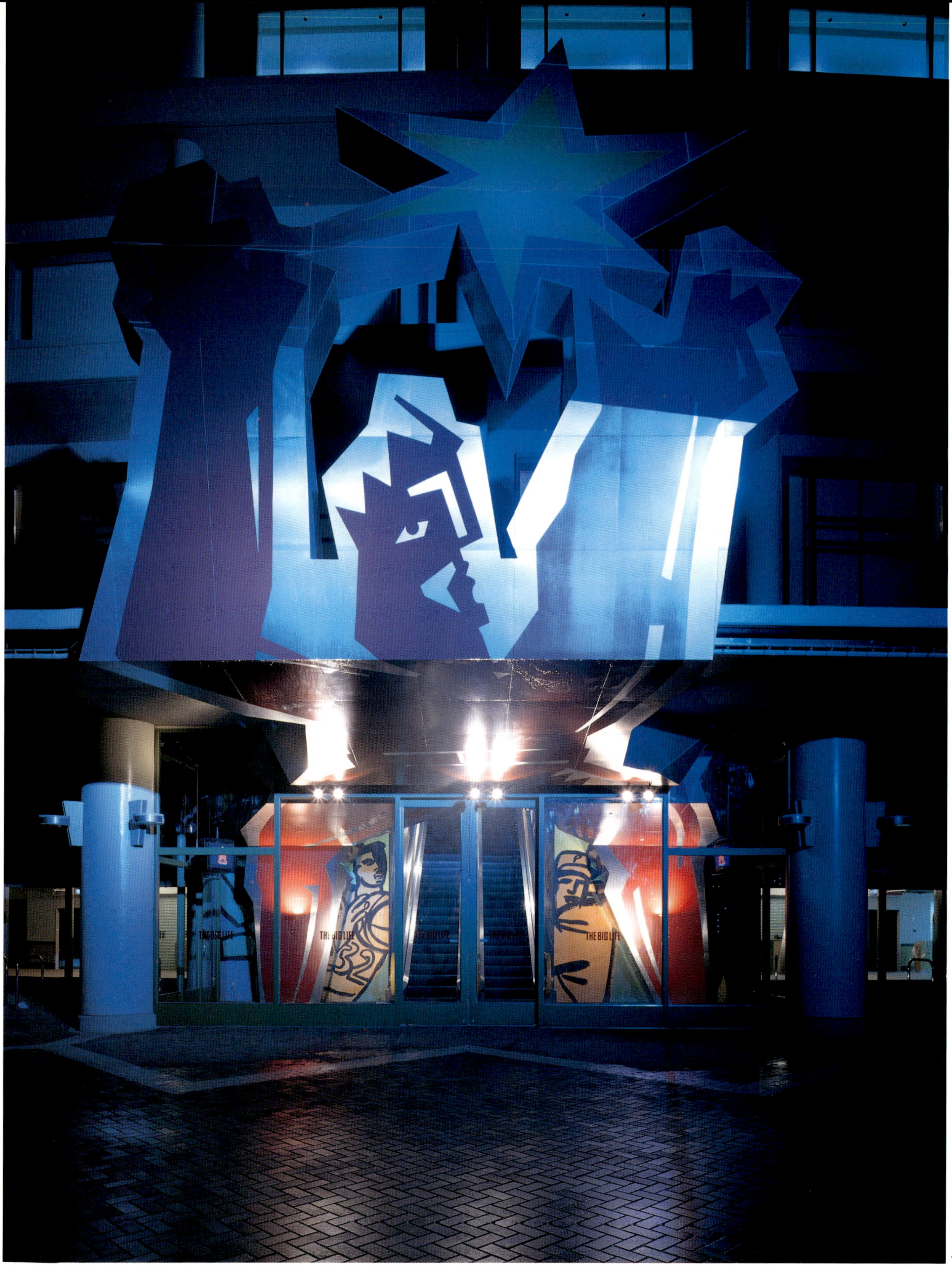

1

野球も観戦できる全長188mのスポーツバー

ザ・ビッグ・ライフ

福岡県福岡市中央区地行浜2丁目2-2 福岡ドーム4階

Sports Bar THE BIG LIFE

Jigyohama Chuo-ku Fukuoka, Producer Shi Yu Chen

プロデュース／CIA シー・ユー・チェン
設計／シュワイツァー・ビーム ジョッシュ・シュワイツァー
アートディレクション／スタジオ・セイリーニ リック・セイリーニ
設備設計・内装施工／イチケン

1. 福岡球場の3階デッキレベルに設けられた入り口夜景
Night view of the entry from the deck
2. 入り口よりエスカレーターで4階の店内へと導かれる
View of the escalator from The 7th Wave area

2

THE BIG LIFE
ALL AMERICAN SPORTS BAR
THE BIG LIFE
THE BIG LIFE
HOME RUN
ILLEGAL
MOTION

3

●アメリカの'50年代モダニズムを蘇らす
福岡ドームは，九州の中心・福岡市の海岸に面してできた屋内型の野球場であり，巨大さと天井の開閉するシステムが人気をよび，多くの人々を集めている。このスポーツバーは野球場の外野席沿いに設けられたもので188メートルの長さをもつ。
このスポーツバーのコンセプトは，野球の試合の行われていない場合でもスポーツ好きの人々を集める魅力のあること，集まった人々が１時間1000円以内の金額で楽しめることであった。細長い円弧を描いた2534m²の店舗は，カーレース，ボート，ボクシングなど17のテーマに分割され，明確な差異化とキャラクター化が図られた。
内部のデザインはアメリカ人の建築家の手になるもので，スポーツマインドに溢れたイラストレーションと運動用具を家具化したオリジナルなデザインによって，コストパフォーマンスとクリエイティビティを両立させた空間を生み出している。

THE BIG LIFE
The Fukuoka dome is an indoor baseball stadium, facing the seacoast of Fukuoka city. Its gigantic scale and opening dome roof attracts a lot of people. This sports bar is situated along the out-field bleachers and the length is 188m.
Requirement for the design was creating a attractive space to draw guests who were not interested in sports and entertaining them on low budgets of less than ¥1,000 per hour. The site was arc-shaped narrow space of 2,534 square meters. There are 17 areas with each design theme such as racing cars, boats, boxing, etc. and each character was clearly designed.
The interior was designed by an American architect. The sports illustrations and furniture made upon forms of sports goods show good cost performance and creativity of the designer.

3. 球場の外野席に沿って設けられたカウンター席
View of the counter and baseball ground
4. カラオケルームのあるエンドゾーン内部
Interior view of the End Zone area
5. 格闘技をテーマとしたバー・リングサイド
Interior view of the Ringside Bar

4

5

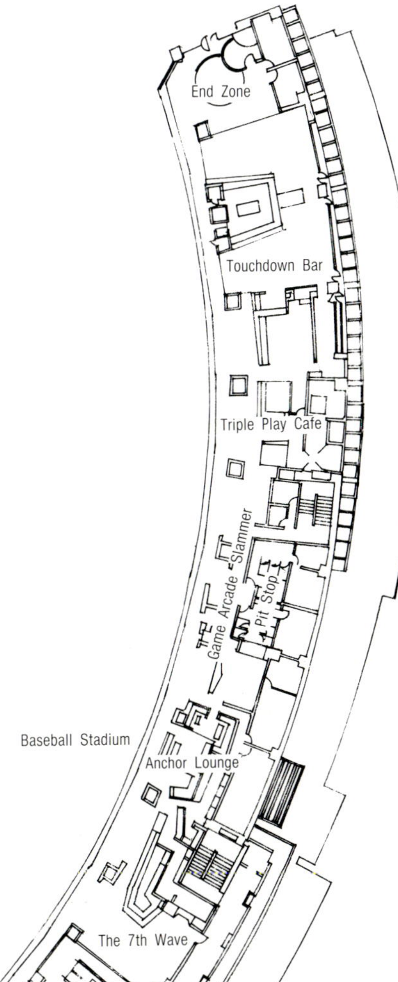
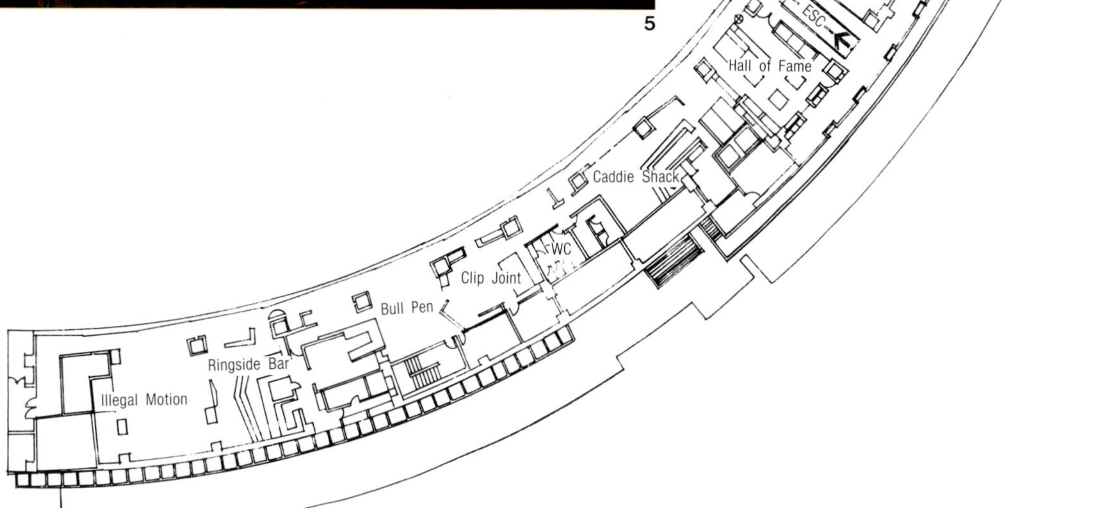

THE BIG LIFE PLAN 1:800

期間限定の仮設スポーツカフェ&ブティック

原宿フープタウン

東京都渋谷区神宮前4丁目31-9

Sports Complex Harajuku HOOPTOWN

Jingumae Shibuya-ku Tokyo, Designer Hiroyuki Ohtsu

●一体感を生み出す金網とビルボード

アメリカのシカゴやニューヨークのダウンタウンには，ビルの谷間にストリートバスケットのコートが点在し，若者たちがスポーツを楽しむ。もちろん正規の大きさのコートではなく，3人ずつが同じバスケットのゴールリングへシュートを放つ“スリーオンスリー”とよばれるゲームである。

東京・原宿にできたこの18カ月の期間限定スポーツカフェは，小人数で，しかも狭い面積で手軽にできるこのゲームを中心に企画された。ビルの外壁はビルボードとよばれるイラストのパネルが取り付けられ，夜間はライトアップされることにより，ガラス張りで内部が透けて見えるコートとともに，自立した中間領域としての存在と建築の力強さを表現している。内部空間もハードな金網をコートとの仕切りに使うことによって，コート空間と各ショップは内でもなく外でもない中間的領域として混じり合い，訪れる客が同じ音を聞き，空気を感じ，一体としての場を共有できる工夫がなされている。

HOOPTOWN

American cities, for example Chicago and New York, are studded with numerous basketball courts. Some people play irregular game like “Three-On-Three” whose players are three and shoot to one goal. This sports cafe in Harajuku is open for limited term of 18 months and it targets mostly players of “Three-On-Three”, making the most of small site and trendy location to attract young people.

The exterior wall has billboard panels with illustrations on them and it is lit up at night, so the interior court is seen from the outside. This project displays itself as an independent medium zone by strong architectural expressions. Wire fences between the court and shop area do not separate the two and both areas share the same active and sporting air of basketball games.

1. 明治通り側から見た西側外観全景
Night view from the west

2. ホットドッグレストランよりコート方向を見る
1F: View of the Hot dog restaurant

1

2

企画／東急エージェンシー
設計／福井・楠美建築設計事務所
大津博之　吉田悦子
協力／積水ハウス
ナイキ・デザイン
ブラッド・バーマン　ジョン・ノーマン
施工／建築　清水ハウス
内装　トライアングル商業施設
エアーズ・ロックエンタープライズ

3

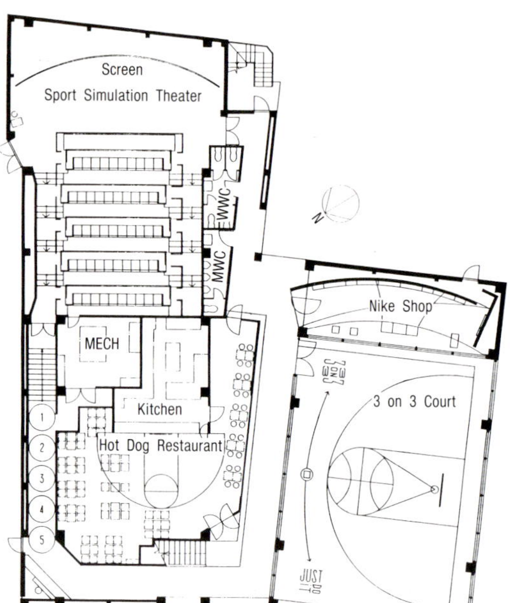

HOOPTOWN 1F PLAN 1:400

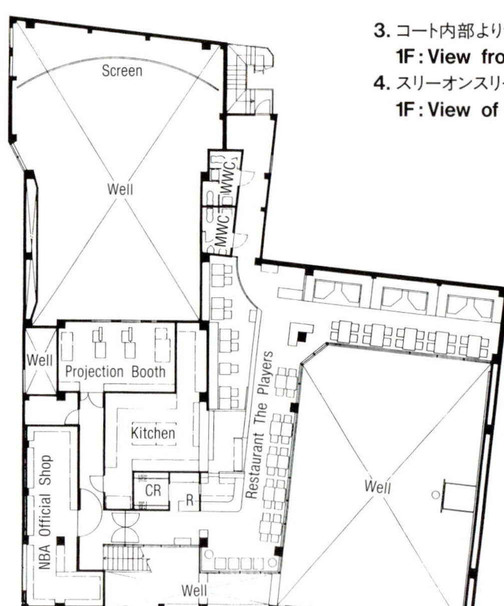

2F PLAN

3. コート内部よりナイキショップ方向を見る
1F: View from the court to the Nike shop
4. スリーオンスリーのゲームを楽しむプレーヤーたち
1F: View of the court and players

JOLT COLA
COLA
B A S K E T

過去の記憶と現代の情報信号を対比させたカフェ

UCCカフェプラザ 新宿店

東京都新宿区新宿3丁目1-16 安田火災海上新宿別館1階

Coffe Shop UCC CAFE PLAZA

Shinjuku Shinjuku-ku Tokyo
Designer Kenji Komoriya

設計／小森谷賢二 ヴィンチ
施工／寿屋木工

1. 道路側外部よりウインドーごしに客席Aを見る
View of the seatings A from the street

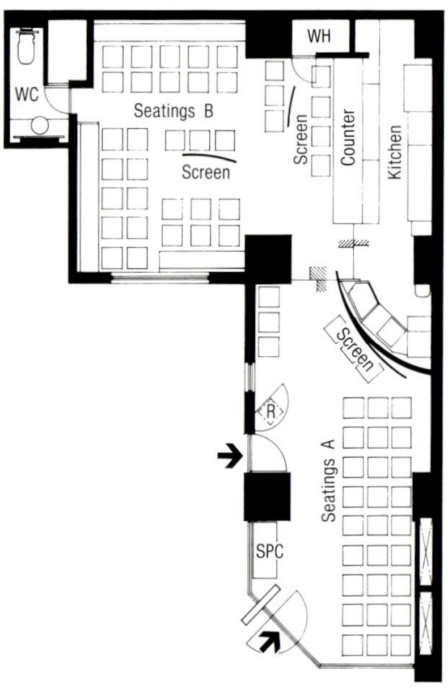

UCC CAFE PLAZA PLAN 1:200

1

3

●不協和音をおこすグリーンの信号

珈琲専門店といえば，濃い茶色の木の梁，塗り壁といった類型的なパターンのデザインが，ほとんどを占めている。東京・新宿の繁華街にあるこの珈琲店も，以前は従来の典型的な珈琲専門店のスタイルであったが，改装を機会に新しいイメージのコーヒーショップへと変身した。

クライアントは大手コーヒーメーカーであるので，メーカーの直営店としての品格，伝統といったものを守りながら，なおかつ新しい要素を採り入れ，これからのカフェのありかたを提案することが要望された。このためデザインは，既存のレンガを柱まわりに残し，また，ない場合は他の壁から撤去されたレンガを積むことから始まった。

レンガは改装前の店舗の記憶であり，柱まわりを取り囲む周囲の空間には，新たに現代的な要素としてグリーンという，情報をイメージさせる信号としての色が配された。新たなグリーンはスクリーンや壁面のオブジェとして，光ったり，曲がったり，変形したりしながら，空間の中で不協和音をおこし，新宿らしい混乱した気分を空間に漂わせている。

2. 入り口側客席Aからカウンター席方向を見る
View from the seatings A to the counter
3. カウンター側から見た客席B全景
View of the seatings B from the counter

UCC CAFE PLAZA

Not a few cafes in this country specializes in serving almost only coffee and designed by stereotype style, using dark brown wood beams and painted walls, etc.
This cafe in downtown Shinjuku used to be such a typical coffee specialist cafe, and it was totally changed into a new type.
As the owner was a major coffee manufacturer, a designer had to give a touch of elegance and tradition to create the new type, fitting to the client.
Existing brickwork around columns were left, added some bricks from other parts of old interior, showing a memory of old image of this cafe. Green, symbolizing information and go sign of traffic lights, was chosen for screens and wall decorations in various ways. Green light, curving green, and other differently green are used in many shapes or forms, expressing a chaotic traffic situation of Shinjuku busy streets with a lot of traffic lights.

2

ローテックなリゾート感覚のカフェレストラン

カフェ・ド・マルティニーク

東京都新宿区新宿５丁目17-１

Café de MARTINIQUE

Shinjuku Shinjuku-ku Tokyo
Designer Sakae Miura

企画／草野政博　ガリバー計画
設計／アール・ビジョン　三浦 栄　大橋政善
施工／建築　アルマテック　テクス
　　　内装　アルマテック

1. 布に覆われた吹き抜け空間を2階客席Bより見る
View from the dining B to the dining A and terrace

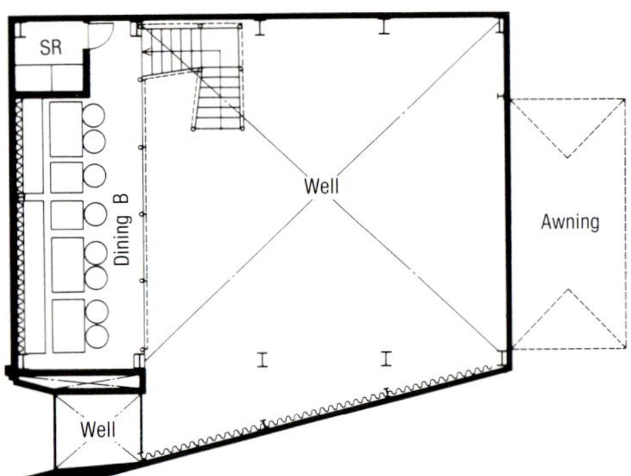

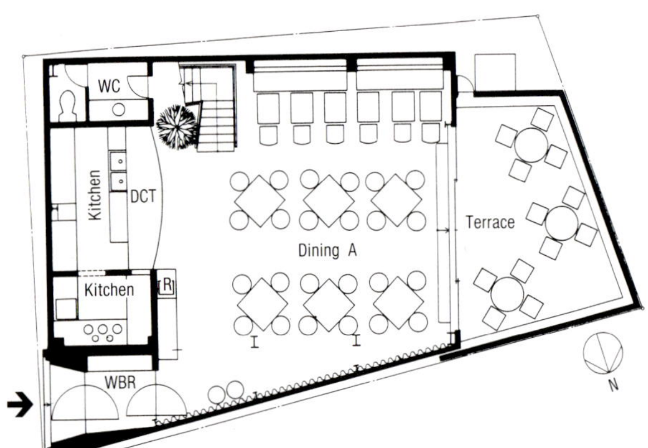

●隣地の自然を取り込んだ開放的空間
東京の代表的な繁華街・新宿は雑多で混沌とした魅力を持ち，活気に溢れた街であるが，そのかわり緑に乏しい。数少ない緑を敷地内に持つ花園神社に面していることから，このカフェレストランは立地を生かし，周囲の緑を採り入れることが企画のコンセプトとされた。
"都市のリゾートカフェ"がテーマとされ，交通量の多い道路に面した外観は閉鎖的で街並みに溶け込んだデザインになっているが，逆に裏側はガラス張りの大きな開口部が設けられ，外部にテラス席なども配されて，隣地の豊かな緑を生かした開放的な雰囲気となっている。
デザインのもう一つの特徴は，工業的な安い素材を使ってリゾート的な空間を演出していることである。壁面の大きな布によるドレープと鏡，床のラフな足場板がヨーロッパの海辺にあるリゾートを連想させ，また，テラス席上部のテントはヨットの帆をイメージしたもので，非日常的な世界を大都会の一隅に現出させている。

MARTINIQUE

Shinjuku, one of typical downtown in Tokyo is a town of mess but it is active and attractive. It has a little green. This restaurant faces a green of the Hanazono Shrine and uses it as a part of design element for the interior.

The main theme of design is a resort cafe in a city. Although the exterior looks closed fronting a busy street, the interior has big openings, a terrace dining area, and seems to be refreshing with neighboring green. Using industrial low-cost material is one characteristic of this project, which eventually contributes to make resort air in the project.

Big drapes on the wall and naturally rough wood floors are from images of a European seaside resort. A tent above the terrace is a sail of yacht, giving guests the precious time to enjoy resort feeling produced on this corner of a city.

雑誌キャンペーンのための情報発信型仮設カフェ

カフェ ミラノ

東京都渋谷区神宮前４丁目31-９

Caffé Milano

Jingumae Shibuya-ku Tokyo
Designer Hiroyuki Tsujinaka

企画／トレイン インターナショナル　長谷川康之
設計／スピン　辻中浩佑
協力／建築申請　アーキシーン　中島信吾
　　　家具コーディネート　石川恵津子
　　　壁画　高藤由明　片桐頼継
　　　グラフィック　アークアソシエーツ
施工／たかのは

1. 明治通りに面した書き割り的なファサードを見る
View of the facade from the street
2. センタードームより奥のキッチン方向を見る
View from the center dome to the kitchen side

1

2

●絵画的手法による舞台装置空間
東京のような大都市では遊休地を有効に活用することは，土地所有者にとっても，一時的使用者にとっても有益なことである。若者の集まるファッションの街・原宿に3カ月という期間限定で，この仮設カフェは作られた。女性のための就職情報雑誌が10周年を記念したキャンペーンの一環として行ったもので，読者と直接にコミュニケーションを持ち，就職情報を提供できる場として企画された。
テレビCFのイメージと連動させるため，テーマは"ミラノ"とされ，ミラノ固有の文化イメージが舞台装置的手法で具現化された。中世，ルネサンス，バロックなどの建築様式をモチーフに新しい要素が加味され，空間が形成されているが，その中でも重要なポイントとなっている壁画やだまし絵（トロンプ・ルイユ）には，美術プロデューサーや多くの画家が参加し，完成度の高いものになっている。4〜6月という穏やかで気持ちの良い季節にふさわしいオープンエアのカフェには，情報を求めて若い女性が集まり，コーヒーを楽しみ，そしてキャンペーンの目的は達せられた。

MILANO
It is useful for landlord and tenants to make the most of idle land in a big city like Tokyo. This temporary cafe opened for three months contract term in Harajuku, a trendy town for young people. It was the part of campaign of the 10th anniversary of a women's magazine to provide the readers information to get jobs.
To link with a TV. commercial, this project was named MILANO and designed like Milanese style stage art, taking motifs from the Middle Age, Renaissance, Baroque and other period styles. Particularly trompe l'oeil work was perfectly designed by an art producer and many painters.
Suitable for mild seasons from April to June, this cafe drew a lot of young women and they enjoyed themselves over coffee, so the campaign attained its goal.

3

3. 奥の厨房側よりセンタードームを通して入り口側を見る **View from the kitchen side to the center dome**

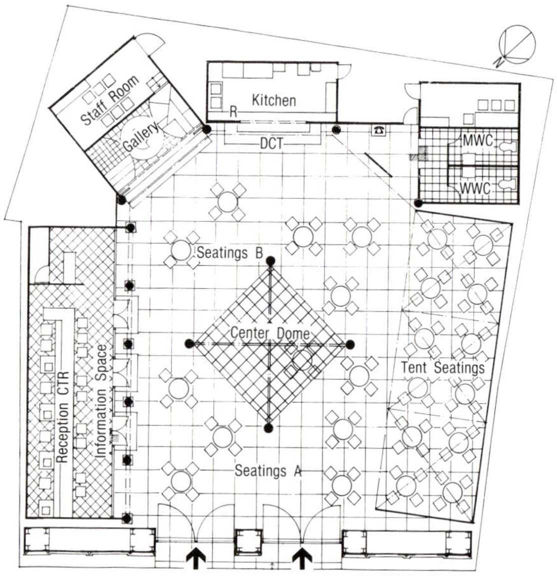

MILANO PLAN 1:300

竹づくしのカフェ&ギャラリー

イースト ギャラリー

東京都渋谷区東３丁目24-７ ライビルディング１階

Café & Gallery East Gallery

Higashi Shibuya-ku Tokyo, Designer Edward Suzuki

設計／鈴木エドワード建築設計事務所
施工／親和工業

1. 本物の竹が植えられたテラス席より受付方向を見る
View from the terrace to the reception counter

1

3

●先端的な建築構造を家具に生かす

このカフェとギャラリーが一体化した空間を設計したのは建築家であり，デザインのテーマは建築家らしく“テンション・インテグリティー”という構造の方法を意匠に採り入れている。引っ張りと圧縮の混合システムを意味するこの方法は，未来志向で有名な建築構造技術者であるバックミンスター・フラーが提案したもので，特徴は圧縮材がおのおの触れ合わず引っ張り材によって形態が固定されるところにある。自然界においては，ミクロの世界で原子核の回りに飛ぶ電子の仕組み，マクロでは太陽系などの軌道がこの構造を表している。

客席に置かれたテーブルは，竹筒を使った3本の脚がこの構造によるものであり，また天井やカウンターの腰部分，パーティションなどには竹筒が使われ，まさに竹づくしの空間である。竹材は使われないままこの空間に積み上げられていたものを利用したものであり，その結果，工事費は非常にローコストで完成した。

2. 竹で構成された受付カウンターの腰部分
Detail of the reception counter
3. 店内奥より入り口方向全景を見る
Whole view from the kitchen entry

2

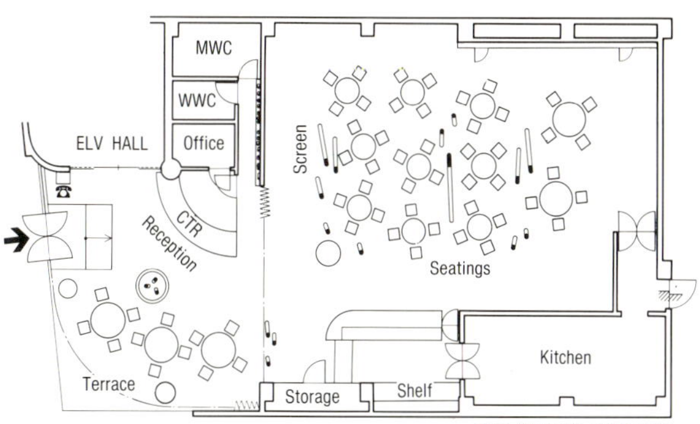

EAST GALLERY PLAN 1:300

EAST GALLERY

An architect designed this cafe and gallery upon his construction theory and method called "Tension Integrity", which means literally a conception of tension and compression and originally proposed by an American architect Backminster Fuller. The point of the theory is that tension members fix a form when compression members do not touch one another. The same type construction can be seen in both micro and macro level in nature nucleus and electron or the solar system, for example.

Three table legs made of bamboos were constructed by the theory.

Bamboos were also used for the ceiling, sides of a counter, and partitions. This project was completed by low cost, as it used bamboos which had been deserted and accumulated in a space.

ポアン デュ ジュール

東京都渋谷区笹塚1丁目9-10

Accessory & Café
POINT DU JOUR

Sasazuka Shibuya-ku Tokyo
Designer Hiroki Michishita

設計／イマジン　道下浩樹
施工／イマジン+アルテコーポレーション

1. レジわきより湾曲したカウンターと客席を見る
View of the counter from the cashier

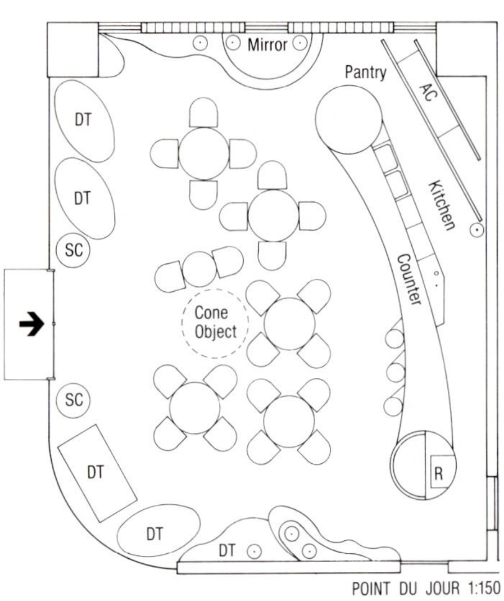

POINT DU JOUR 1:150

1

2

●フランス的な香りのする空間
この店のオーナーはフランスが好きで，しばしば訪れては気に入ったアクセサリーその他を買い集め，日本で販売している。5店目になるこの店は，東京・笹塚にあり，アクセサリーだけでなく，カフェを併設することでショールーム的な意味合いを付加している。また，地下1階にカルチャースクールをオープンするにあたり，やってくる人々のためのロビー的なコミュニケーションの場としての役割も期待された。
デザインのコンセプトは，何々風といったものではなく，オーナー自身のパーソナリティーとフランス的な香りが意識され，分かりやすく，馴染みやすい表現が心掛けられた。伸び伸びと柔らかく弧を描いた水平に広がるラインに対して，ピシッとした真っ直ぐの垂直の線。これらにより構成された空間造形を彩る様々な温かい明かりは，ほのぼのとした中にも一本筋の通った心地良い緊張感を内部空間にもたらしている。

2. パントリー側壁面のミラーに映り込んだ虚像
The virtual image of the wall mirror

POINT DU JOUR
The owner of this store loves France and often go there to purchase accessories and sell them in Japan. This shop in Sasazuka, Tokyo is the fifth store for the owner and it has a cafe, where customers enjoy saloon atmosphere. The basement has a open class for adult education. This store was planned for the students to use as a lounge.
The design concept was not strictly defined but it represented owner's character and French taste. It is simple and friendly.
Smooth and gentle arcs are used horizontally and strong straight lines are characteristic with soft lighting. Heartwarming air and agreeable tension fill the interior.

駅構内の待ち合わせ場所としてのカフェテリア

ア ポイント

東京都千代田区丸の内1丁目9-1 東京駅八重洲南口

Cafeteria A POINT

Marunouchi Chiyoda-ku Tokyo, Planner Mitsuhiro Ono

企画／ピロタージュ　小野光洋　丸笠昌司
設計／ア・ファクトリー
施工／建築　ゼニヤプランニングオフィス　内装　ア・ファクトリー

1. JR東京駅の公共通路より見た外観。ガラス張りで内部がよく見える構造となっている
View of the facade from the public passage

1

●古い駅の風景を現代風にアレンジ
カフェテリアは，客がメニューを選んでレジで代金を支払い，料理をセルフサービスでテーブルまで運んで食べるというスタイルで，アメリカで発達したシステムである。しかし，日本では今まで大学の学生食堂や企業の社員食堂以外には，あまり普及しなかった。セルフサービスの割には価格が安くない，料理を長時間にわたり保温しておくので美味でないなどの理由からであろう。東京駅の構内にできたこのカフェテリアは，食事だけでなく，巨大で複雑な駅の待ち合わせの場所として企画された。従来は駅の一角にシンボル的なものを置いただけの広場しかなかったが，ここで待ち合わせれば混雑することもなく，コーヒーを飲みながら落ち着いた気分で待つことができるというわけだ。
このような意図から，外観デザインは外から内部がよく見えるようにガラス張りとされ，また，内部空間は古い駅のイメージを基本に温か味のあるボンヤリとした雰囲気を意図し，料理や客が映えるように照明や素材も配慮されている。

2. 入り口右側の客席Bより見た1階客席全景
View from the seatings B to the kitchen

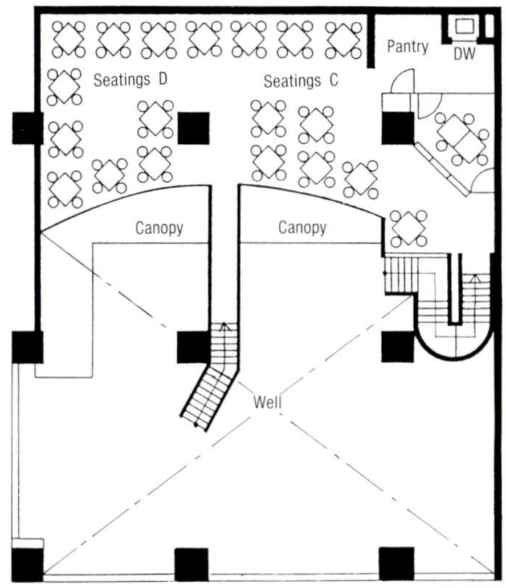

2F PLAN

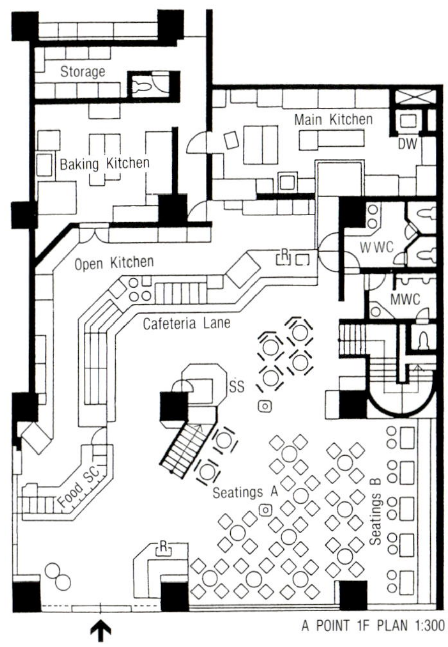

A POINT 1F PLAN 1:300

2

A POINT
Cafeterias were developed in the U.S. for people to choose easily their favorite food and pay at cashiers by themselves. In Japan, cafeterias are not so popular except those in colleges and companies, for the cost is unexpectedly expensive and people do not like so much the self-help system. It may be natural that anyone would not like so much foods kept warming for long time by machine, because the taste will becomes stale.
This cafeteria in Tokyo station was planned as not only an eatery but also a waiting place. Usually in Japan, waiting places in stations are just corners or areas with or without some markers or sculptural objects. This cafe and waiting room, however, caters to people's comfortable area for relaxation over coffee.
The exterior are glazed and the interior looks warm and old-fashioned. Based upon an image of an old station. Lighting and materials were carefully chosen to show food and guests nicely.

11の屋台で構成された空港のセルフサービスカフェ

ラ・フィェスタ

千葉県成田市新東京国際空港 第2旅客ターミナルビル4階

Restaurant LA FIESTA

Narita-Airport Narita-shi Chiba, Designer WORKSHOP

1

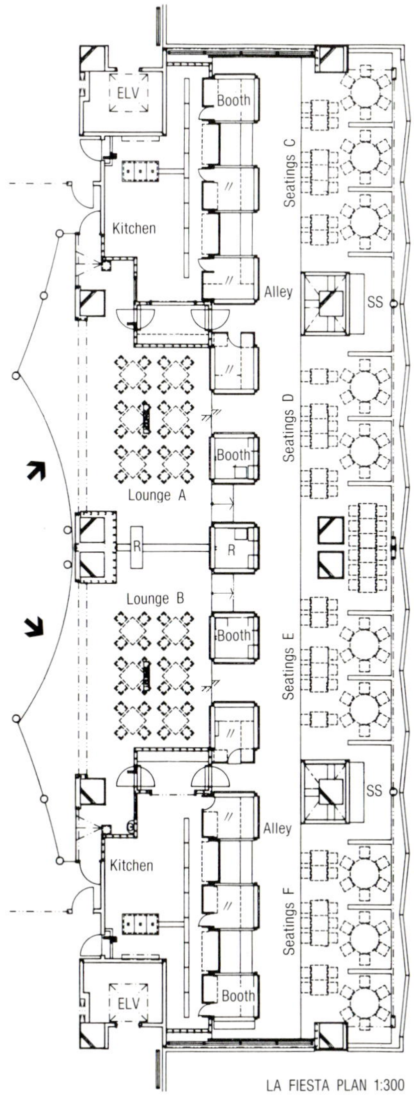

LA FIESTA PLAN 1:300

設計／ワークショップ
協力／郷設計　施工／千葉三越

1. 店内中央のレジわきより左側アレイ（通路）方向を見る
View of the Alley from the cashier side

2

●屋台の賑やかさと便利さを採り入れる
空港で出国を待つ旅行者は，一分でも早く搭乗準備を終え，余裕のある心もちでスタンバイしたいものである。したがってカフェテリア形式のスピーディなレストランには最適な立地といえよう。しかし従来の空港内レストランは高くて，まずいというのが常識であり，客は他に施設がないため，あきらめて利用するというパターンがほとんどであった。
日本の玄関口・成田空港に新しくできた旅客ターミナル内のこのレストランは，それらの欠点を克服し，現状を打破することから企画はスタートした。ポイントとなったのは，11台のブースと呼ばれる屋台で，料理のジャンル別に分かれ，客は好みのメニューのあるブースへ行けば，作り置きではなく，一分以内というスピードで調理される作りたての料理を受け取ることができる。
細長い形状の店内は，アレイとよばれる通路でブースの列と客席に分けられ，客はこの通路を歩きながら色とりどりのバナーでメニューが表示されたブースから好みの料理を選択し，スピーディに受け取ることができるのである。

2. 左奥客席Cより屋台風ブース方向を見る
View of the Booths from the seatings C

LA FIESTA
Travelers need to sit themselves on chairs in waiting rooms in relaxed atmosphere, soon after they finish boarding procedures. For this reason, there must be a convenient cafeteria in airports. However, we know that most airport restaurants are expensive and the food is not tasty, so we often do not expect nice eateries there.
This restaurant in Narita airport, a door to Tokyo, was planned to break travelers' common sense, offering good food and service. In this restaurant, eleven booths ("yatai" in Japanese) for different foods which are cocked on the spot for people to pay quickly. The narrow interior is divided by a passage called "alley" into two zones. Visitors can browse here and there, strolling the long passage decorated by banners of booths.

"不思議の国のアリス"をテーマにしたファストフード

アリスのテーブル

大分県別府市城島高原123 城島後楽園ゆうえんち内

Fast Food Restaurant ALICE'S TABLE

Kijimakogen Beppu-shi Oita
Designer Takenaka Corporation

設計・施工／竹中工務店九州支店
協力／コムデザインアソシエイツ

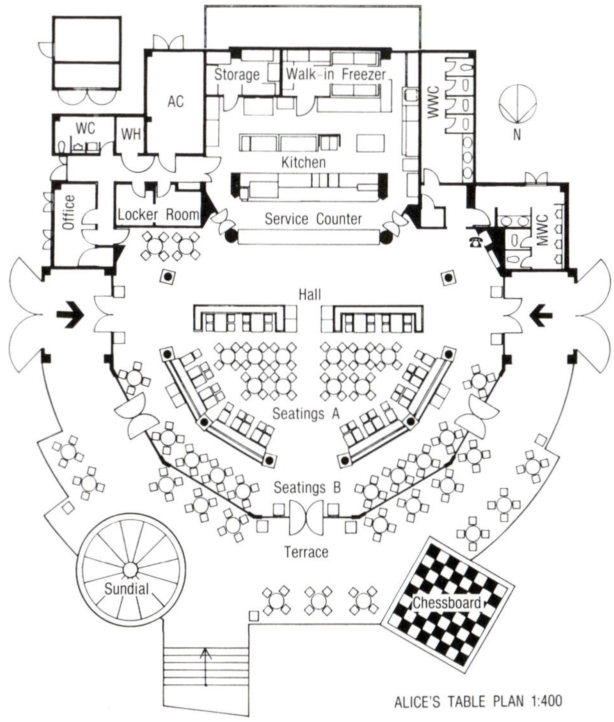

ALICE'S TABLE PLAN 1:400

1. 遊園地内にある建物を西側より見た夜景
Night view from the west side to the entry

1

●地中の穴をイメージした天井デザイン
遊園地には子供たちだけでなく，童心に帰った大人たちを楽しませる仕掛けや施設が必要である。特に手軽に利用できるファストフードレストランは，食事をすると同時に休憩の場所でもあるので，遊園地の印象を決定する重要な場所といえる。
九州・別府市の郊外に立地する遊園地にできたこのファストフードのレストランは，有名な童話"不思議の国のアリス"がテーマである。物語の主人公であるアリスが，白うさぎのあとを追って入りこんだ地下の不思議な国での大冒険をモチーフにした空間で，穴の中というイメージを演出するため高さ8メートルの天井高が設定された。同心円状に配置された天井のパーティションは中央にいくに従って高くなり，中心部分の明るく塗られた色彩と照明の効果により，地中の穴から空を見た感覚が再現されている。また，中央の天井から吊られた歓迎サインには白うさぎが配され，その周囲にはトランプの兵隊をイメージしたバナーが吊り下げられ，来園した客たちを迎える。

2. テラス側の客席Bより厨房方向を見た全景
View of the interior from the seatings B

ALICE'S TABLE
Amusement parks are for both kids and adults with innocent mind, so they have to have also facilities for adults. Fast food restaurants are essential for amusement parks and sometime represent faces of the parks, since visitors have their meals and have a break there.
This fast food restaurant in Beppu city in Kyushu Island was designed upon a concept of Lewis Carroll's nursery tale "Alice's Adventures in Wonderland". The interior represents Alice's world which she reached, going through a hole and following a white rabbit.
An 8m high ceiling makes visitors feel like they are in the bottom of the hole. The ceiling decoration panels are arranged in a concentric circle, the outer panels are bigger than the inner ones. To express the contrast of the outside and inside the underground world, the colors of the decorative panels have gradation in colors inner ones are brighter than outer ones. So, visitors imagine the sky is beyond the center of the ceiling. Welcome signs of white rabbits are hanging from the ceiling and "playing card soldiers" are printed on banners.

2

WELCOME TO
ALICE'S TABLE
Teriyakiburger
Cheeseburger
DESSERTS
TOILET

茶菓をメーンとした京都の老舗和菓子喫茶

みずは北川 祇園店

京都府京都市東山区南座東隣り 志満家ビル1階

Confectionery & Café
MIZUHA KITAGAWA

Minamiza-higashidonari Higashiyama-ku Kyoto
Designer Takao Kawasaki

企画／北川 明 河崎隆雄 潮 宏樹 G.S.P.
設計／カワサキ・タカオ・オフィス
河崎隆雄 潮 宏樹
施工／G.S.P. アート・リキ

●中庭の役割を果たす吹き抜け空間
長い歴史と伝統を持つ京都の街には，茶道に使われる茶菓を中心にした和菓子の老舗が多くあり，京都の人々は茶を嗜みながら茶菓を食べるのが楽しみの一つである。南座という古い劇場の隣にあるこの和菓子喫茶は，劇場の改築に合わせて改修され，和菓子を販売するだけでなく，奥のコーナーに2層の喫茶客席が設けられた。
京都の町家は間口が狭く，奥行きが長い鰻の寝床状の敷地が多いが，この店も同様の形状をしている。道路に面した1階入り口には和菓子を実際に作っている実演コーナーが設けられ，その背後に和菓子の売り場がある。さらにその奥のブリッジを渡った部分が喫茶客席で，ブリッジわきの吹き抜け空間ごしに地下1階のもう一つの喫茶客席が見える。この吹き抜けは，町家の中庭にあたる部分で，高い天井と相まって開放的な雰囲気を空間にもたらしている。また，1階と地下1階客席の床に貼られた割りタイルは，階によって色が変えられ，デザインに微妙な変化を与えている。

1

1. 吹き抜け側より1階右奥客席方向を見る
View of the seatings A
2. レジわきより見た1・2階客席※
View of the seatings A and B

MIZUHA KITAGAWA
In Kyoto, an old capital with the long history and tradition, there are old stores dealing traditional confectionery for tea ceremony. Sipping tea everyday, people in Kyoto like to eat such sweet things. Minamiza, an authentic theater, is next to this old Japanese confectionery store. When the theater was renovated, the store was also renewed, added two story level tea lounge in the back. Most of traditional Kyoto town houses have small entrance and prolonged sites, which are called "houses of eels", and so does this store.
There is a demonstration corner near the entrance to show how they make their authentic sweet things. Passing through the shop area and going further over a bridge, visitors find a tea lounge on the first floor and another in the basement through a void which is located where there are usually a court in this type of town house. The high ceiling gives a open feeling to the tea lounge. Broken tiles are used for the tea lounge and the color scheme are different for each floor.

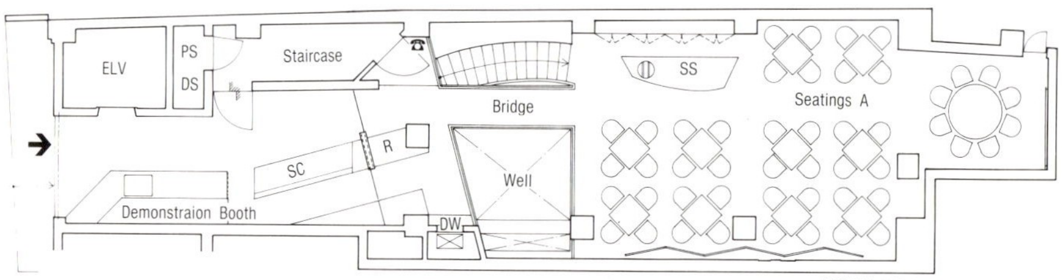

MIZUHA KITAGAWA 1F PLAN 1:200

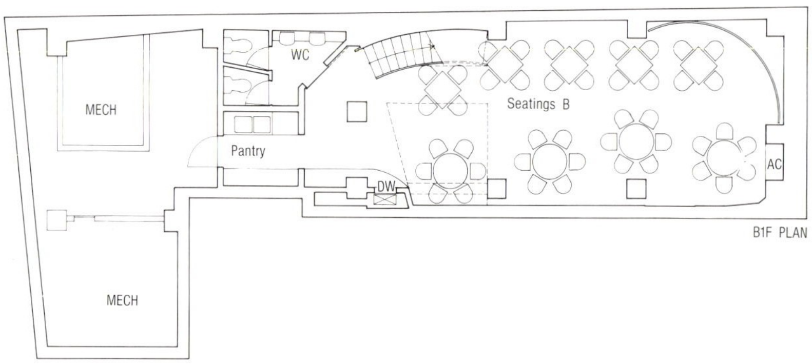

B1F PLAN

洋風菓子と和風空間を融合させたチーズケーキ・カフェ

フロマージュウ

京都府向日市寺戸町初田19-3 K&Cプラザ2階

Pâtisserie & Café FROMAGE

Terado-cho Muko-shi Kyoto, Designer Isamu Nakamura

1

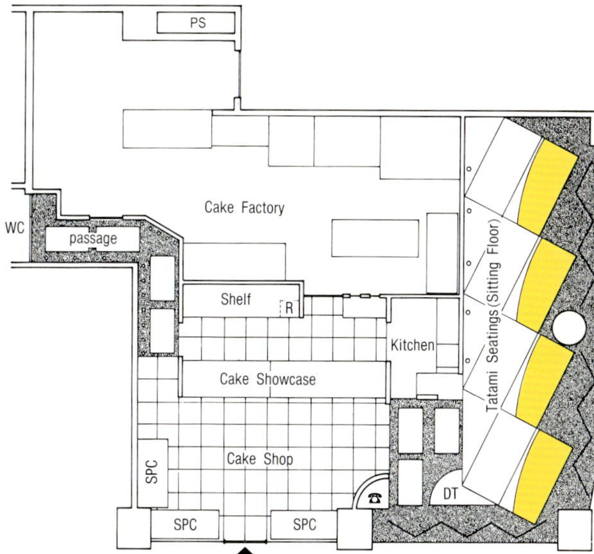

FROMAGE PLAN 1:150

2

設計／中村勇大アトリエ　中村勇大
協力／グラフィックデザイン　梅宮弘光
施工／ファッシーノ

1. 右奥コーナー客席より入り口方向を見る
View of the Tatami seatings from the inner part
2. ケーキ売り場よりトイレへ至るアプローチ通路
View of passage from the cake shop to the lavatory

3

●工業的素材による和風表現
チーズケーキは西洋の食べものであり，ケーキをメーンにした洋菓子喫茶店は，西洋的なデザインで空間が構成されているのが通常である。京都の郊外にできたこの洋菓子喫茶は，常識とは違って，日本的な要素と意匠を大胆に採り入れているのが特徴である。
ケーキ売り場からトイレに至る通路は，小石が敷き詰められ，飛び石を模したグレーチングが配されている。また，試食を兼ねたカフェコーナーにも同様に小石が敷かれ，日本的なものの象徴として置かれた"畳"の上に座り，屏風をモチーフとしたスクリーンに囲まれながら客は飲食を楽しむ。
しかし，日本的な意匠といっても空間に使われているのは伝統的な素材ではなく，たとえば，壁や天井にはメッキされた鋼板の平板や小波板，飛び石と樹を模したポールにはステンレスが使われている。これらの工業的な部材による"和"の新しい表現は，異なる文化を対比させると同時に融合させ，今までにない斬新な空間デザインを生み出している。

3. ケーキ売り場より客席の上がり口まわりを見る
View of the seatings from the cake shop

FROMAGE
Cheese cakes, needless to say, one of Western confectionery and cake shops are usualy designed by the Western style in Japan.
Different from ordinary cake shops, this one in a suburb of Kyoto was designed boldly using Japanese style and design elements.
A passage floor from shop area to rest rooms are covered with small stone with quasi-stepping stones in grating.
A cafe corner's floor is also covered with small stone. Visitors sit and enjoy eating and drinking in a tatami mats area with a folding screen in the back.
Although the interior design looks Japanese but the material is not traditional. Gilded steel panels and short pitch corrugated sheets are used for walls and the ceiling. Stepping stones and plant-like objects are stainless steel. With these industrial material parts, a new Japanese style and unique spatial design was created, contrasting and combining different cultures.

ディナー&テーマレストラン

ザ ガーデン・データ(P6)

工事種別：内装のみ　新築
床面積：1885㎡(うち厨房563㎡)
工期：1991年9月1日〜1992年1月31日
総工費：10億円(植栽費1億円含む)
●営業内容
開店：1992年3月5日
営業時間：午前11時30分〜午後2時　午後5時30分〜午後10時30分(ラストオーダー午後9時30分)
定休日：日曜日　電話：(03)5404-4050
経営者：㈱ガーデンレストランシステム
従業員：サービス17人　厨房2人　パート・アルバイト常時66人　合計85人
客席数：487席
客単価：6000〜7000円　客回転数：1回
主なメニューと単価：コース料理4000〜　アラカルト800〜　ビール600〜　カクテル800〜
●主な仕上げ材料
外壁：熱線吸収ガラス
サイン：ネオンサイン
床：大理石貼り　粘板岩タイル貼り　ナラ材&ブナ材　フローリング貼り
幅木：モルタル幅木　H100，150
壁：PBｔ21二重貼り下地AEP　一部壁画仕上げ
天井：軀体のまま　一部トップライト　特殊散水システム取り付け
照明器具：HQI+HID混光照明　ハロゲンランプ　シリカ球ほか
家具：特注テーブル
植栽：超薄型人工地盤植栽システム(スーパーリソール工法／クレアテラ)　植栽樹木／ガジュマル　ベンジャミン　犬ビワ　ユズリハ　ソテツ　ヤツデ　竹ほか
●撮影：ナカサ&パートナーズ('92年5月号)

東京バモラ・データ(P12)

工事種別：一戸建て　新築
用途地域地区：準工業地域　防火地域
建ぺい率：制限70%>実効38.38%
容積率：制限441.96%>実効441.27%　(共にオフィス棟を含む)
構造と規模：S+SRC造　一部RC造　地下1階　地上3階建て
敷地面積：5445.22㎡
建築面積：2089.64㎡(オフィス棟含む)
床面積：1階846㎡　2階464㎡　合計1310㎡
工期：1990年11月2日〜1993年2月15日
●営業内容
開店：1993年4月2日
営業時間：
ランチタイム・午前11時〜午後3時　ティータイム・午後2時〜午後5時　ディナータイム・午後5時〜午後11時
定休日：なし　電話：(03)5454-7007
経営者：㈱レストランテ・バモラ
従業員：サービス103人　厨房56人　合計159人
客席数：516席　客回転数：2.5回
客単価：1階バー／7800円　1階シーフードレストラン／5000円　2階ブラジルレストラン／4000円
主なメニューと単価：1階バー／カレーなる白身魚400　タラモ玉入れ競争550　1階シーフードレストラン／ストーンクラブクロー2980　豪快!!ステーキ&ロブスター2980　2階ブラジルレストラン／シュラスコセット2900　シュラスココース4000　ビール430　ワイン1500
●主な仕上げ材料
屋根：アスファルト断熱防水砂利押さえ
外壁：アルミカーテンウオール電解発色　透明フロートガラス　中空押し出し成型セメント板シリコン樹脂塗装
外部床：アスファルト断熱防水のうえ磁器タイル貼り200角
サイン：スチールメラミン焼き付け
床：色コンクリート表面加工(ボーマクロン工法／永代機械工業)　コンパネ下地カリン材フローリングｔ17
壁：PB下地エマルション系塗材(ジョリパット／アイカ工業)コテ仕上げ　丸柱／プラスター下地アンティーク塗装　PB下地ジョリパット吹き付け　銅板腐食仕上げ
天井：PB下地AEPおよびジョリパット吹き付け
家具・什器：ナラ材OFおよびブビンガ材OF
●撮影：飯嶋祐司('93年6月号)

アミエル&フリスコ・データ(P16)

企画：㈱ライカ開発課
工事種別：内装のみ　新築
床面積：1階326.74㎡(厨房を除く)　地下1階595.82㎡　合計922.56㎡
工期：1989年9月15日〜11月30日
●カフェ営業内容
開店：1990年1月8日
営業時間：午前10時〜午後6時
定休日：なし　電話：(06)614-5589
経営者：㈱ライカ
従業員：サービス3人　厨房2人　パート・アルバイト3人　合計8人
客席数：80席　客単価：500円
主なメニューと単価：コーヒー350　紅茶350　フレッシュジュース700　フルーツフローズン500　アミーズ(ケーキセット)600　アミエルデザート700　ロングドリンク450
●レストラン営業内容
開店：1990年4月上旬
電話：(06)614-5590　客席数：170席
●主な仕上げ材料
床：1階／テラゾタイル400角(テラタイル・フェレグラニット／アドヴァン)および島崎石乱貼り　およびカーペット敷き　地下／テラゾタイル400角および黒御影石乱貼りジェットバーナー仕上げ　目地人工芝および特注パーティクルボード600角
壁：軀体のまま　一部地下／ブビンガ化粧合板貼り　1階／米松合板貼り
天井：地下／PBｔ12模様吹き付け塗材(ジョリパット／アイカ工業)　1階／PBｔ12アクリル系吹き付け塗材(ラフトン／鈴鹿塗料)
パーティション&大テーブル：フロストガラススパッタリング加工
照明：地下／間接照明(ルニエース／ニッポ電機)　1階／FLあんどん照明
テーブル：特殊テラゾブロックｔ50本磨き
●撮影：山田誠良('90年3月号)

レストラン サトー・データ(P21)

工事種別：内装のみ　全面改装
床面積：120.50㎡(うち厨房21.10㎡)
工期：1990年9月24日〜1991年1月31日
●主な仕上げ材料
床：石灰岩貼り400角水磨き(バルシー／テーチーエム東京)
壁：軽鉄組みPBｔ12下地寒冷紗パテシゴキ砂入りスタッコ(スタッコ・アンティコ／エバーファースト)　雪見障子／杉田杉ウレタン塗装
天井：軽鉄組みPBｔ12下地寒冷紗パテシゴキVP
パーティション：大分産真竹染色乱れ編み
カウンター：黒御影石本磨き　腰／バルシー貼り水磨き
テーブル：セン合板ウレタン塗装　脚／スチールメラミン焼き付け塗装
イス：カッシーナジャパン　YMD
●撮影：ナカサ&パートナーズ('91年8月号)

東京ディナー・データ(P24)

工事種別：一戸建て　新築
用途地域地区：住居地域　商業地域　防火地域　準防火地域
建ぺい率：制限78.20%>実効54.27%
容積率：制限202.10%>実効197.78%
構造と規模：RC造　地下1階　地上3階建て
敷地面積：288.13㎡　建築面積：170.75㎡
床面積：地下1階218.93㎡　1階101.06㎡　2階155.00㎡　3階94.88㎡　合計569.87㎡(うち厨房61.6㎡)
工期：1990年6月5日〜1992年6月26日
●営業内容
開店：1992年7月5日
営業時間：ランチタイム／午前11時30分〜午後2時　ティータイム／午後2時〜午後5時　ディナータイム／午後5時〜9時30分
定休日：なし
電話：(03)5420-4001　経営者：喜代幸平
従業員：サービス12人　厨房10人　合計22人
客席数：90〜100席　客回転数：1回
客単価：ランチ3000円　ディナー1万〜1万5000円
主なメニューと単価：ランチコース2500〜　ディナーコース7500〜　ビール800　コーヒー650　グラスワイン700
●主な仕上げ材料
屋根：RC歩行用アスファルト防水コンクリート金ゴテ押さえ
外壁：RC下地骨材入り色シックイ掻き落とし　スチールサッシ　強化ガラスタペストリー加工　アルミサッシ網入りガラスFIX　オークムク板ワトコオイル仕上げ
外部床：砂利洗い出し　一部大理石タイル貼り(チョットリ／志野陶石)
床：モルタル下地サクラ材フローリング　テラコッタタイル貼り(バルセロナ／エヌティーシー)
幅木：サクラ材　H100　H30
壁：モルタル下地骨材入り色シックイくし引き仕上げ　一部掻き落としおよびスタンピング仕上げ　モルタル下地プラスター塗り　ボード下地サクラ材練り付けウレタンCL
天井：PBｔ9AEP　モルタル下地プラスター仕上げ
照明器具：ピンホールダウンライト(遠藤照明)　ピンスポット(ヤマギワ)　ハロゲンスポット(パラボラックス／ヤマギワ)
家具：サクラ材練り付けステイン着色ウレタンCL
●撮影：ナカサ&パートナーズ('92年9月号)

ボーセジュール&エトワール・データ(P28)

工事種別：ファサードと内装　新築
床面積：ボーセジュール／311㎡(うち厨房197㎡)　エトワール／360㎡(厨房は兼用)
工期：1988年9月26日〜1991年8月30日(建築含む)
●営業内容
開店：1991年9月5日
営業時間：ボーセジュール／午後5時〜午後10時　エトワール／午前11時〜午前2時
定休日：なし　電話：(0492)27-1111
経営者：㈱プリンスホテル
客席数：ボーセジュール／64席(個室2室)　エトワール／102席(個室2室)
主なメニューと単価：ボーセジュール／ディナー1万　1万2000　エトワール／カクテル800〜　スコッチウイスキー(S)800〜
●主な仕上げ材料
〈ボーセジュール〉
床：コンクリート下地フローリングダブルヘリンボーン貼り　大理石ボーダー　真鍮見切り　個室／カーペット敷き
幅木：桜材染色CL　H120
壁：軽鉄組みPBｔ9+PBｔ12下地AEP　大理石貼り　桜材染色CL
天井：トップライト+グラスファイバー製電動ロールスクリーン金箔模様押し
照明器具：特注シャンデリア
〈エトワール〉
床：コンクリート下地フローリング貼り　大理石貼り
幅木：セン材染色　H110
壁：軽鉄組みPBｔ9+PBｔ12下地AEP
天井：軽鉄組みPBｔ9下地AEP
照明器具：ダウンライト
●撮影：鈴木　光('92年2月号)

ベルダンテュール・データ(P31)

工事種別：一戸建て　新築
用途地域地区：近隣商業地域
建ぺい率：制限80%>実効71.7%
容積率：制限300%>実効126.7%
構造と規模：RC造(1階)+木造(2階)
敷地面積：131.0㎡　建築面積：93.9㎡
床面積：1階88.6㎡(うち厨房44.4㎡)　2階77.4㎡　合計166.0㎡
工期：1989年1月10日〜5月14日
●営業内容
開店：1989年5月24日
営業時間：午前11時〜午後10時
定休日：火曜日　電話：(0899)43-7776
経営者：ピア企画　高橋順子
従業員：サービス6人　厨房5人　パート・アルバイト常時3人　合計14人
客席数：60席
客単価：5000円　客回転数：2回
主なメニューと単価：ディナー3500〜7000　シェフのおすすめ1万〜　ランチ1500〜3500　食談メニュー2500〜4500　パーティーメニュー5000　ア・ラ・カルト700〜
●主な仕上げ材料
屋根：ラワン合板下地石綿スレート葺き(カラーベストコロニアル／クボタ)

作品データ

外壁：防火サイディング貼りVP　一部ラスモルタル下地二丁掛けタイル　トップライト／スチールサッシュアルミラッカー焼き付け　網入り透明ガラスｔ8
外部床：モルタル下地玉石洗い出し　一部御影石ジェットバーナーウレタン塗装
床：モルタル下地ナラフローリング直貼り　一部カーペット敷き　玉石洗い出し　一部大理石
壁：PBｔ12AEP　腰／シナ合板木材保護着色塗装(キシラデコール／武田薬品工業)
天井：PBｔ12AEP　化粧染／米松キシラデコール塗装
●撮影：大竹静市郎('90年5月号)

天王洲倶楽部・データ(P34)

工事種別：内装のみ　新築
床面積：4400㎡
工期：1992年9月1日〜1993年3月5日
総工費：9億円
●営業内容
開業：1993年4月27日
営業時間：イタリアンプロヴァンス料理・日本料理／午前11時30分〜午後3時　午後5時〜午後10時30分　バー／午後5時〜午後11時　カフェテラス／午前11時〜午後6時　リラクセーションフロア／午前11時〜午後10時
定休日：日曜日　電話：(03)5462-0200
経営者：スフィアコーポレーション
従業員：サービス9人　厨房13人　パート・アルバイト8人　合計30人
客単価：5500円　客回転数：1.2回
主なメニューと単価：イタリアンプロヴァンス料理／ランチ1800 2500 5000　ディナー5000 7800 1万　日本料理／昼食2500 4500　夕食8000　1万2000　1万5000　バー／ウイスキー1000〜　カクテル各種1000〜　カフェテラス／コーヒー700　ケーキ各種700　リラクセーションフロア／法人会員　1000(登録料100万　年間負担金90万)　ビジター　9000
●主な仕上げ材料
床：コンクリート下地大理石貼り(トラバーチン)　コンパネｔ25下地フローリング　カーペット貼り
壁：PBｔ12二重貼りスタッコ塗装およびEP
天井：PBｔ12EP　スチールプレートｔ1.2 OP　回り縁／プラスターの上にEP
●撮影：野口　毅('93年7月号)

テラス モルチェ・データ(P38)

工事種別：内装のみ　新築
床面積：457㎡(うち厨房140㎡)
工期：1992年11月1日〜1993年3月15日
●営業内容
開店：1993年5月15日
営業時間：午前10時〜午後9時
電話：(03)3446-2581　経営者：㈱中央亭　磯野謙蔵
従業員：サービス9人　厨房9人　パート・アルバイト常時2人　合計20人
客席数：110席
客単価：2000円　客回転数：6回
主なメニューと単価：ランチコース2400　パスタ1500〜1600　ベジタブルバー1500　デザート600　樽黒生ビール(ジョッキ)900
●主な仕上げ材料
床：軽量コンクリート下地ホワイトオークフローリング　一部染色処理　花崗岩貼り(モンシーク)
幅木：ホワイトオークおよび花崗岩　H100
壁：軽鉄組みPB下地AEP　化粧リブ材AEP(ニューファッションリブ／サカイ)　タモ染色練り付け不燃板
天井：軽鉄組みPB下地化粧岩綿吸音板パターン貼り(ソーラトンストライプ／日東紡績)
家具：テーブル(フリッツハンセンB-403／アクタス)　イス(フリッツハンセン3101)
●撮影：冨田　治('93年7月号)

サーフ&ターフ・データ(P42)

工事種別：ファサードと内装　全面改装
床面積：475.2㎡(うち厨房98.02㎡)
工期：1991年9月1日〜1992年1月25日
総工費：1億3000万円
解体撤去費250万円　内装造作費4700万円　空調設備費850万円　厨房設備費1500万円　給排水衛生設備費250万円　電気設備費800万円　照明器具費1100万円　家具・什器費2600万円　音響設備費100万円　壁画300万円　その他550万円
●営業内容
開店：1992年2月5日　定休日：なし
営業時間：午前11時〜午前0時
電話：(0899)43-3138
経営者：㈱天壇　玉井重明
従業員：サービス2人　厨房2人　パート・アルバイト常時5人　合計9人
客席数：レストラン165席 バー16席 合計181席
客単価：2500円　客回転数：2回
主なメニューと単価：日替わりランチ680　サーモンステーキ1200　シーフードサラダ850　ニューヨークステーキセット2650　スペアリブセット1200　ビール500
●主な仕上げ材料
外壁：モルタル下地OP(米国製塗料)　ガラス質タイル貼り(ベニーガラスモザイク330／アドヴァン)
外部床：コンクリート下地磁器質タイル乱貼り150角(イナックス)
サイン：銅板腐食仕上げ
床：コンクリート下地磁器質タイル乱貼り150角　ガラス質タイル貼り　木床／メープル合板クリア塗装
壁：木下地プラスター塗りOP特注ワックス仕上げ　パーティション／銅板ウロコ貼り　マホガニー材染色
天井：PBｔ12下地OP特注ワックス仕上げ　梁／木下地プラスター塗りOP特注ワックス仕上げ
照明器具：アルミ＋銅板
家具：バーカウンター／ナラ材染色
●撮影：武市基靖('93年1月号)

FBI・データ(P46)

工事種別：一戸建て　新築
用途地域地区：指定なし　市街化調整区域
建ぺい率：制限50%>実効14.5%
容積率：制限なし>実効22.9%
構造と規模：S造　地上2階建て
敷地面積：4962.19㎡　建築面積：721.68㎡
床面積：1階709.58㎡(うち厨房160.00㎡)　2階428.99㎡　合計1138.57㎡
工期：1991年7月1日〜12月21日
総工費：4億5660万円
建築軀体工事費2億7000万円　サイン550万円　空調・給排水衛生設備費5000万円　厨房設備費3700万円　電気設備費6280万円　家具費1100万円　ロースター770万円　ビール釜据え付け・運搬費1260万円
●営業内容
開店：1991年12月24日
営業時間：午前11時〜午後11時
定休日：なし　電話：(096)368-0800
経営者：アイセック㈱
従業員：サービス4人　厨房5人　パート・アルバイト常時30人　合計39人
客席数：430席
客単価：2800円　客回転数：1.6回
主なメニューと単価：ジンギスカン食べ飲み放題2913　シュラスコ食べ放題2800　FBIコロッケ650　ラムシャブ食べ飲み放題3300　コーヒー350　60cm超ロングソーセージ1300　生ビール(中)400
●主な仕上げ材料
屋根：木毛セメント板ｔ20(センチュリーボード／三井木材工業)　アスファルトルーフィング下地カラー鉄板ｔ0.6(トーカイカラー／東海鋼業)一文字葺き
外壁：古レンガ一枚積み(都窯業)　カラーアルミサッシ　スチール製ドア　スチール形鋼サッシ
外部床：外構／透水性カラー舗装およびコンクリート舗装ブロック300角　ポーチ／モルタルコテ押さえ　フロアタイル300角(スパニッシュ／名古屋モザイク工業)
床：モルタル金ゴテ押さえ下地スパニッシュ300角パターン貼り　モルタル金ゴテ押さえ下地真鍮目地化粧スチール格子埋め込み　スチールチェッカードプレート400角ｔ4.5埋め込み　枕木150×250　南洋材プレーナー仕上げOSCL　2階ブリッジ／スチールチェッカードプレート　手摺り・スチールフラットバー
壁：古レンガ積み(都窯業)　一部樹脂入りプラスター木ゴテ押さえ(マジックコート／フッコー)
天井：PBｔ12下地マジックコート木ゴテ押さえ　一部アンティークペイント　ビアタンク席：ビアタンク銅板研磨ウレタン塗布
●撮影：砂川敏夫('92年4月号)

ルドルフ バーベキュー・データ(P50)

工事種別：一戸建て　新築
用途地域地区：商業地域　防火地域
建ぺい率：制限100%>実効75.36%
容積率：制限600%>実効126.03%
構造と規模：S造　地上2階建て
敷地面積：547.90㎡　建築面積：412.92㎡
床面積：1階412.92㎡(うち厨房108.20㎡)　2階277.59㎡(うち厨房36.67㎡)　合計690.51㎡(うち厨房144.87㎡)
工期：1992年5月1日〜10月31日
●営業内容
開店：1992年11月17日
営業時間：午前11時〜午前0時　定休日：なし
電話：(06)281-0091　経営者：㈱ココリコ
従業員：サービス6人　厨房5人　パート・アルバイト常時20人　合計31人
客席数：200席　客単価：昼750円　夜2200円
客回転数：2回
主なメニューと単価：ランチ(7品)650〜1500　ザ・アラモ(ビーフスペアリブ)2800　サンセットブルバード(セットメニュー)1800　コーヒー330　生ビール(S)430
●主な仕上げ材料
屋根：軽量コンクリートアスファルト防水の上モルタル金ゴテ仕上げ　網入りガラスｔ6.8
外壁：ALC板ｔ100下地古レンガ貼り(深川建材工業)　一部リシン吹き付け
外部床：古レンガ貼り
サイン：アルミ板ｔ6メラミン焼き付け　ネオン
床：コンパネｔ12下地ナラ材フローリング貼り染色クリアワックス仕上げ　モザイクタイル貼り25角　パティオ／テラコッタタイル貼り(プロバンス／TGM東京)　クリアコート樹脂ワックス仕上げ
幅木：アガチス材AEP　H60
壁：PBｔ12下地目地寒冷紗総パテシゴキAEP
天井：PBｔ12下地目地寒冷紗総パテシゴキAEP
家具：椅子(ササビー)　テラス椅子(スパゲッティチェア／インターデコール)　特注家具(佐山製作所)
●撮影：軍司隆博('93年7月号)

ファミール シナネン店・データ(P53)

工事種別：内装のみ　新築
床面積：419.76㎡(うち厨房112.00㎡)
工期：1992年11月20日〜1993年1月12日
●営業内容
開店：1993年5月6日
営業時間：午前11時〜午後9時
定休日：土曜・日曜・祭日
電話：(03)5463-9478　経営者：㈱ファミール
従業員：サービス4人　厨房8人　パート・アルバイト常時8人　合計20人
客席数：143席(カウンター7席)
客回転数：2回
客単価：ランチ600円　アイドルタイム300円　パブタイム1700円
主なメニューと単価：ランチ580　630　茶そば400　ハンバーグステーキ750　冷奴280　串カツ480　ケーキ380　コーヒー290　ビール480
●主な仕上げ材料
床：モルタル金ゴテ下地磁器タイル貼り300角(バルセロナ／NTC)　塩ビタイル貼り(メルウッド／東リ)
幅木：ブナ材染色CL　H35
壁：PBｔ12下地AEPローラー　スクリーン／タペストリーガラス　柱形／ボンデ鋼板＋PBｔ12下地AEP
天井：PBｔ9下地AEPローラー
●撮影：ナカサ&パートナーズ('93年7月号)

インコントロ・データ(P56)

工事種別：ファサードと内装　全面改装
床面積：レストラン370.96㎡(うち厨房84.00㎡)　ホール549.40㎡　合計920.36㎡
工期：1989年7月20日〜10月7日
●営業内容
開店：1989年10月8日
営業時間：午前11時30分〜午後11時
定休日：なし　電話：(03)3708-6161
経営者：日本中央開発㈱
従業員：サービス8人　厨房12人　合計20人

ディナー&テーマレストラン

ザ ガーデン・データ(P6)

工事種別:内装のみ 新築
床面積:1885㎡(うち厨房563㎡)
工期:1991年9月1日〜1992年1月31日
総工費:10億円(植栽費1億円含む)
●営業内容
開店:1992年3月5日
営業時間:午前11時30分〜午後2時 午後5時30分〜午後10時30分(ラストオーダー午後9時30分)
定休日:日曜日 電話:(03)5404-4050
経営者:㈱ガーデンレストランシステム
従業員:サービス17人 厨房2人 パート・アルバイト常時66人 合計85人
客席数:487席
客単価:6000〜7000円 客回転数:1回
主なメニューと単価:コース料理4000〜 アラカルト800〜 ビール600〜 カクテル800〜
●主な仕上げ材料
外壁:熱線吸収ガラス
サイン:ネオンサイン
床:大理石貼り 粘板岩タイル貼り ナラ材&ブナ材 フローリング貼り
幅木:モルタル幅木 H100,150
壁:PBt21二重貼り下地AEP 一部壁画仕上げ
天井:軀体のまま 一部トップライト 特殊散水システム取り付け
照明器具:HQI+HID混光照明 ハロゲンランプ シリカ球ほか
家具:特注テーブル
植栽:超薄型人工地盤植栽システム(スーパーリソール工法/クレアテラ) 植栽樹木/ガジュマル ベンジャミン 犬ビワ ユズリハ ソテツ ヤツデ 竹ほか
●撮影:ナカサ&パートナーズ('92年5月号)

東京バモラ・データ(P12)

工事種別:一戸建て 新築
用途地域地区:準工業地域 防火地域
建ぺい率:制限70%>実効38.38%
容積率:制限441.96%>実効441.27% (共にオフィス棟を含む)
構造と規模:S+SRC造 一部RC造 地下1階 地上3階建て
敷地面積:5445.22㎡
建築面積:2089.64㎡(オフィス棟含む)
床面積:1階846㎡ 2階464㎡ 合計1310㎡
工期:1990年11月2日〜1993年2月15日
●営業内容
開店:1993年4月2日
営業時間:
ランチタイム・午前11時〜午後3時 ティータイム・午後2時〜午後5時 ディナータイム・午後5時〜午後11時
定休日:なし 電話:(03)5454-7007
経営者:㈱レストランテ・バモラ
従業員:サービス103人 厨房56人 合計159人
客席数:516席 客回転数:2.5回
客単価:1階バー/7800円 1階シーフードレストラン/5000円 2階ブラジルレストラン/4000円
主なメニューと単価:1階バー/カレーなる白身魚400 タラモ玉入れ競争550 1階シーフードレストラン/ストーンクラブクロー2980 豪快!!ステーキ&ロブスター2980 2階ブラジルレストラン/シュラスコセット2900 シュラスココース4000 ビール430 ワイン1500
●主な仕上げ材料
屋根:アスファルト断熱防水砂利押さえ
外壁:アルミカーテンウオール電解発色 透明フロートガラス 中空押し出し成型セメント板 シリコン樹脂塗装
外部床:アスファルト断熱防水のうえ磁器タイル貼り200角
サイン:スチールメラミン焼き付け
床:色コンクリート表面加工(ボーマクロン工法/永代機械工業) コンパネ下地カリン材フローリングt17
壁:PB下地エマルション系塗材(ジョリパット/アイカ工業)コテ仕上げ 丸柱/プラスター下地アンティーク塗装 PB下地ジョリパット吹き付け 銅板腐食仕上げ
天井:PB下地AEPおよびジョリパット吹き付け
家具・什器:ナラ材OFおよびブビンガ材OF
●撮影:飯嶋祐司('93年6月号)

アミエル&フリスコ・データ(P16)

企画:㈱ライカ開発課
工事種別:内装のみ 新築
床面積:1階326.74㎡(厨房を除く) 地下1階595.82㎡ 合計922.56㎡
工期:1989年9月15日〜11月30日
●カフェ営業内容
開店:1990年1月8日
営業時間:午前10時〜午後6時
定休日:なし 電話:(06)614-5589
経営者:㈱ライカ
従業員:サービス3人 厨房2人 パート・アルバイト3人 合計8人
客席数:80席 客単価:500円
主なメニューと単価:コーヒー350 紅茶350 フレッシュジュース700 フルーツフローズン500 アミーズ(ケーキセット)600 アミエルデザート700 ロングドリンク450
●レストラン営業内容
開店:1990年4月上旬
電話:(06)614-5590 客席数:170席
●主な仕上げ材料
床:1階/テラゾタイル400角(テラタイル・フェレグラニット/アドヴァン)および島崎石乱貼り およびカーペット敷き 地下/テラゾタイル400角および黒御影石乱貼りジェットバーナー仕上げ 目地人工芝および特注パーティクルボード600角
壁:軀体のまま 一部地下/ブビンガ化粧合板貼り 1階/米松合板貼り
天井:地下/PBt12模様吹き付け塗材(ジョリパット/アイカ工業) 1階/PBt12アクリル系吹き付け塗材(ラフトン/鈴鹿塗料)
パーティション&大テーブル:フロストガラス スパッタリング加工
照明:地下/間接照明(ルニエース/ニッポ電機) 1階/FLあんどん照明
テーブル:特殊テラゾブロックt50本磨き
●撮影:山田誠良('90年3月号)

レストラン サトー・データ(P21)

工事種別:内装のみ 全面改装
床面積:120.50㎡(うち厨房21.10㎡)
工期:1990年9月24日〜1991年1月31日
●主な仕上げ材料
床:石灰岩貼り400角水磨き(バルシー/テーヂーエム東京)
壁:軽鉄組みPBt12下地寒冷紗パテシゴキ砂入りスタッコ(スタッコ・アンティコ/エバーファースト) 雪見障子/杉田杉ウレタン塗装
天井:軽鉄組みPBt12下地寒冷紗パテシゴキVP
パーティション:大分産真竹染色乱れ編み
カウンター:黒御影石本磨き 腰/バルシー貼り水磨き
テーブル:セン合板ウレタン塗装 脚/スチールメラミン焼き付け塗装
イス:カッシーナジャパン YMD
●撮影:ナカサ&パートナーズ('91年8月号)

東京ディナー・データ(P24)

工事種別:一戸建て 新築
用途地域地区:住居地域 商業地域 防火地域 準防火地域
建ぺい率:制限78.20%>実効54.27%
容積率:制限202.10%>実効197.78%
構造と規模:RC造 地下1階 地上3階建て
敷地面積:288.13㎡ 建築面積:170.75㎡
床面積:地下1階218.93㎡ 1階101.06㎡ 2階155.00㎡ 3階94.88㎡ 合計569.87㎡(うち厨房61.6㎡)
工期:1990年6月5日〜1992年6月26日
●営業内容
開店:1992年7月5日
営業時間:ランチタイム/午前11時30分〜午後2時 ティータイム/午後2時〜午後5時 ディナータイム/午後5時〜9時30分
定休日:なし
電話:(03)5420-4001 経営者:喜代幸平
従業員:サービス12人 厨房10人 合計22人
客席数:90〜100席 客回転数:1回
客単価:ランチ3000円 ディナー1万〜1万5000円
主なメニューと単価:ランチコース2500〜 ディナーコース7500〜 ビール800 コーヒー650 グラスワイン700
●主な仕上げ材料
屋根:RC歩行用アスファルト防水コンクリート金ゴテ押さえ
外壁:RC下地骨材入り色シックイ掻き落としスチールサッシ 強化ガラスダペストリー加工 アルミサッシ網入りガラスFIX オークムク板ワトコオイル仕上げ
外部床:砂利洗い出し 一部大理石タイル貼り(チョットリ/志野陶石)
床:モルタル下地サクラ材フローリング テラコッタタイル貼り(バルセロナ/エヌティーシー)
幅木:サクラ材 H100 H30
壁:モルタル下地骨材入り色シックイくし引き仕上げ 一部掻き落としおよびスタンピング仕上げ モルタル下地プラスター塗り ボード下地サクラ材練り付けウレタンCL
天井:PBt9AEP モルタル下地プラスター仕上げ
照明器具:ピンホールダウンライト(遠藤照明) ピンスポット(ヤマギワ) ハロゲンスポット(パラボラックス/ヤマギワ)
家具:サクラ材練り付けステイン着色ウレタンCL
●撮影:ナカサ&パートナーズ('92年9月号)

ボーセジュール&エトワール・データ(P28)

工事種別:ファサードと内装 新築
床面積:ボーセジュール/311㎡(うち厨房197㎡) エトワール/360㎡(厨房は兼用)
工期:1988年9月26日〜1991年8月30日(建築含む)
●営業内容
開店:1991年9月5日
営業時間:ボーセジュール/午後5時〜午後10時 エトワール/午前11時〜午前2時
定休日:なし 電話:(0492)27-1111
経営者:㈱プリンスホテル
客席数:ボーセジュール/64席(個室2室) エトワール/102席(個室2室)
主なメニューと単価:ボーセジュール/ディナー1万 1万2000 エトワール/カクテル800〜 スコッチウイスキー(S)800〜
●主な仕上げ材料
〈ボーセジュール〉
床:コンクリート下地フローリングダブルヘリンボーン貼り 大理石ボーダー 真鍮見切り 個室/カーペット敷き
幅木:桜材染色CL H120
壁:軽鉄組みPBt9+PBt12下地AEP 大理石貼り 桜材染色CL
天井:トップライト+グラスファイバー製電動ロールスクリーン金箔模様押し
照明器具:特注シャンデリア
〈エトワール〉
床:コンクリート下地フローリング貼り 大理石貼り
幅木:セン材染色 H110
壁:軽鉄組みPBt9+PBt12下地AEP
天井:軽鉄組みPBt9下地AEP
照明器具:ダウンライト
●撮影:鈴木 光('92年2月号)

ベルダンテュール・データ(P31)

工事種別:一戸建て 新築
用途地域地区:近隣商業地域
建ぺい率:制限80%>実効71.7%
容積率:制限300%>実効126.7%
構造と規模:RC造(1階)+木造(2階)
敷地面積:131.0㎡ 建築面積:93.9㎡
床面積:1階88.6㎡(うち厨房44.4㎡) 2階77.4㎡ 合計166.0㎡
工期:1989年1月10日〜5月14日
●営業内容
開店:1989年5月24日
営業時間:午前11時〜午後10時
定休日:火曜日 電話:(0899)43-7776
経営者:ピア企画 高橋順子
従業員:サービス6人 厨房5人 パート・アルバイト常時3人 合計14人
客席数:60席
客単価:5000円 客回転数:2回
主なメニューと単価:ディナー3500〜7000 シェフのおすすめ1万〜 ランチ1500〜3500 食談メニュー2500〜4500 パーティーメニュー5000 ア・ラ・カルト700〜
●主な仕上げ材料
屋根:ラワン合板下地石綿スレート葺き(カラーベストコロニアル/クボタ)

作品データ

外壁：防火サイディング貼りVP　一部ラスモルタル下地二丁掛けタイル　トップライト／スチールサッシュアルミラッカー焼き付け　網入り透明ガラスｔ８
外部床：モルタル下地玉石洗い出し　一部御影石ジェットバーナーウレタン塗装
床：モルタル下地ナラフローリング直貼り　一部カーペット敷き　玉石洗い出し　一部大理石
壁：PBｔ12AEP　腰／シナ合板木材保護着色塗装(キシラデコール／武田薬品工業)
天井：PBｔ12AEP　化粧染／米松キシラデコール塗装
●撮影：大竹静市郎('90年５月号)

天王洲倶楽部・データ(P34)

工事種別：内装のみ　新築
床面積：4400㎡
工期：1992年９月１日〜1993年３月５日
総工費：９億円
●営業内容
開業：1993年４月27日
営業時間：イタリアンプロヴァンス料理・日本料理／午前11時30分〜午後３時　午後５時〜午後10時30分　バー／午後５時〜午後11時　カフェテラス／午前11時〜午後６時　リラクセーションフロア／午前11時〜午後10時
定休日：日曜日　電話：(03)5462-0200
経営者：スフィアコーポレーション
従業員：サービス９人　厨房13人　パート・アルバイト８人　合計30人
客単価：5500円　客回転数：1.2回
主なメニューと単価：イタリアンプロヴァンス料理／ランチ1800 2500 5000　ディナー5000 7800 １万　日本料理／昼食2500 4500　夕食8000　１万2000　１万5000　バー／ウイスキー1000〜　カクテル各種1000〜　カフェテラス／コーヒー700　ケーキ各種700　リラクセーションフロア／法人会員　1000(登録料100万　年間負担金90万)　ビジター　9000
●主な仕上げ材料
床：コンクリート下地大理石貼り(トラバーチン)　コンパネｔ25下地フローリング　カーペット貼り
壁：PBｔ12二重貼りスタッコ塗装およびEP
天井：PBｔ12EP　スチールプレートｔ1.2 OP　回り縁／プラスターの上にEP
●撮影：野口　毅('93年７月号)

テラス モルチェ・データ(P38)

工事種別：内装のみ　新築
床面積：457㎡(うち厨房140㎡)
工期：1992年11月１日〜1993年３月15日
●営業内容
開店：1993年５月15日
営業時間：午前10時〜午後９時
電話：(03)3446-2581　経営者：㈱中央亭　磯野謙蔵
従業員：サービス９人　厨房９人　パート・アルバイト常時２人　合計20人
客席数：110席
客単価：2000円　客回転数：６回
主なメニューと単価：ランチコース2400　パスタ1500〜1600　ベジタブルバー1500　デザート600　樽黒生ビール(ジョッキ)900
●主な仕上げ材料
床：軽量コンクリート下地ホワイトオークフローリング　一部染色処理　花崗岩貼り(モンシーク)
幅木：ホワイトオークおよび花崗岩　H100
壁：軽鉄組みPB下地AEP　化粧リブ材AEP(ニューファッションリブ／サカイ)　タモ染色練り付け不燃板
天井：軽鉄組みPB下地化粧岩綿吸音板パターン貼り(ソーラトンストライブ／日東紡績)
家具：テーブル(フリッツハンセンB-403／アクタス)　イス(フリッツハンセン3101)
●撮影：冨田　治('93年７月号)

サーフ&ターフ・データ(P42)

工事種別：ファサードと内装　全面改装
床面積：475.2㎡(うち厨房98.02㎡)
工期：1991年９月１日〜1992年１月25日
総工費：１億3000万円
解体撤去費250万円　内装造作費4700万円　空調設備費850万円　厨房設備費1500万円　給排水衛生設備費250万円　電気設備費800万円　照明器具費1100万円　家具・什器費2600万円　音響設備費100万円　壁画300万円　その他550万円
●営業内容
開店：1992年２月５日　定休日：なし
営業時間：午前11時〜午前０時
電話：(0899)43-3138
経営者：㈱天壇　玉井重明
従業員：サービス２人　厨房２人　パート・アルバイト常時５人　合計９人
客席数：レストラン165席 バー16席 合計181席
客単価：2500円　客回転数：２回
主なメニューと単価：日替わりランチ680　サーモンステーキ1200　シーフードサラダ850　ニューヨークステーキセット2650　スペアリブセット1200　ビール500
●主な仕上げ材料
外壁：モルタル下地OP(米国製塗料)　ガラス質タイル貼り(ベニーガラスモザイク330／アドヴァン)
外部床：コンクリート下地磁器質タイル乱貼り150角(イナックス)
サイン：銅板腐食仕上げ
床：コンクリート下地磁器質タイル乱貼り150角　ガラス質タイル貼り　木床／メープル合板クリア塗装
壁：木下地プラスター塗りOP特注ワックス仕上げ　パーティション／銅板ウロコ貼り　マホガニー材染色
天井：PBｔ12下地OP特注ワックス仕上げ　梁／木下地プラスター塗りOP特注ワックス仕上げ
照明器具：アルミ＋銅板
家具：バーカウンター／ナラ材染色
●撮影：武市基靖('93年１月号)

FBI・データ(P46)

工事種別：一戸建て　新築
用途地域地区：指定なし　市街化調整区域
建ぺい率：制限50%>実効14.5%
容積率：制限なし>実効22.9%
構造と規模：S造　地上２階建て
敷地面積：4962.19㎡　建築面積：721.68㎡
床面積：１階709.58㎡(うち厨房160.00㎡)　２階428.99㎡　合計1138.57㎡
工期：1991年７月１日〜12月21日
総工費：４億5660万円
建築軀体工事費２億7000万円　サイン550万円　空調・給排水衛生設備費5000万円　厨房設備費3700万円　電気設備費6280万円　家具費1100万円　ロースター770万円　ビール釜据え付け・運搬費1260万円
●営業内容
開店：1991年12月24日
営業時間：午前11時〜午後11時
定休日：なし　電話：(096)368-0800
経営者：アイセック㈱
従業員：サービス４人　厨房５人　パート・アルバイト常時30人　合計39人
客席数：430席
客単価：2800円　客回転数：1.6回
主なメニューと単価：ジンギスカン食べ飲み放題2913　シュラスコ食べ放題2800　FBIコロッケ650　ラムシャブ食べ飲み放題3300　コーヒー350　60cm超ロングソーセージ1300　生ビール(中)400
●主な仕上げ材料
屋根：木毛セメント板ｔ20(センチュリーボード／三井木材工業)　アスファルトルーフィング下地カラー鉄板ｔ0.6(トーカイカラー／東海鋼業)一文字葺き
外壁：古レンガー枚積み(都窯業)　カラーアルミサッシ　スチール製ドア　スチール形鋼サッシ
外部床：外構／透水性カラー舗装およびコンクリート舗装ブロック300角　ポーチ／モルタルコテ押さえ　フロアタイル300角(スパニッシュ／名古屋モザイク工業)
床：モルタル金ゴテ押さえ下地スパニッシュ300角パターン貼り　モルタル金ゴテ押さえ下地真鍮目地化粧スチール格子埋め込み　スチールチェッカードプレート400角ｔ4.5埋め込み　枕木150×250　南洋材プレーナー仕上げOSCL　２階ブリッジ／スチールチェッカードプレート　手摺り・スチールフラットバー
壁：古レンガ積み(都窯業)　一部樹脂入りプラスター木ゴテ押さえ(マジックコート／フッコー)
天井：PBｔ12下地マジックコート木ゴテ押さえ　一部アンティークペイント　ビアタンク席：ビアタンク銅板研磨ウレタン塗布
●撮影：砂川敏夫('92年４月号)

ルドルフ バーベキュー・データ(P50)

工事種別：一戸建て　新築
用途地域地区：商業地域　防火地域
建ぺい率：制限100%>実効75.36%
容積率：制限600%>実効126.03%
構造と規模：S造　地上２階建て
敷地面積：547.90㎡　建築面積：412.92㎡
床面積：１階412.92㎡(うち厨房108.20㎡)　２階277.59㎡(うち厨房36.67㎡)　合計690.51㎡(うち厨房144.87㎡)
工期：1992年５月１日〜10月31日
●営業内容
開店：1992年11月17日
営業時間：午前11時〜午前０時　定休日：なし
電話：(06)281-0091　経営者：㈱ココリコ
従業員：サービス６人　厨房５人　パート・アルバイト常時20人　合計31人
客席数：200席　客単価：昼750円　夜2200円
客回転数：２回
主なメニューと単価：ランチ(７品)650〜1500
ザ・アラモ(ビーフスペアリブ)2800　サンセットブルバード(セットメニュー)1800　コーヒー330　生ビール(S)430
●主な仕上げ材料
屋根：軽量コンクリートアスファルト防水の上モルタル金ゴテ仕上げ　網入りガラスｔ6.8
外壁：ALC板ｔ100下地古レンガ貼り(深川建材工業)　一部リシン吹き付け
外部床：古レンガ貼り
サイン：アルミ板ｔ６メラミン焼き付け　ネオン
床：コンパネｔ12下地ナラ材フローリング貼り　染色クリアワックス仕上げ　モザイクタイル貼り25角　パティオ／テラコッタタイル貼り(プロバンス／TGM東京)　クリアコート樹脂ワックス仕上げ
幅木：アガチス材AEP　H60
壁：PBｔ12下地目地寒冷紗総パテシゴキAEP
天井：PBｔ12下地目地寒冷紗総パテシゴキAEP
家具：椅子(サザビー)　テラス椅子(スパゲッティチェア／インターデコール)　特注家具(佐山製作所)
●撮影：軍司隆博('93年７月号)

ファミール シナネン店・データ(P53)

工事種別：内装のみ　新築
床面積：419.76㎡(うち厨房112.00㎡)
工期：1992年11月20日〜1993年１月12日
●営業内容
開店：1993年５月６日
営業時間：午前11時〜午後９時
定休日：土曜・日曜・祭日
電話：(03)5463-9478　経営者：㈱ファミール
従業員：サービス４人　厨房８人　パート・アルバイト常時８人　合計20人
客席数：143席(カウンター７席)
客回転数：２回
客単価：ランチ600円　アイドルタイム300円　パブタイム1700円
主なメニューと単価：ランチ580　630　茶そば400　ハンバーグステーキ750　冷奴280　串カツ480　ケーキ380　コーヒー290　ビール480
●主な仕上げ材料
床：モルタル金ゴテ下地磁器タイル貼り300角(バルセロナ／NTC)　塩ビタイル貼り(メルウッド／東リ)
幅木：ブナ材染色CL　H35
壁：PBｔ12下地AEPローラー　スクリーン／タペストリーガラス　柱形／ボンデ鋼板＋PBｔ12下地AEP
天井：PBｔ９下地AEPローラー
●撮影：ナカサ&パートナーズ('93年７月号)

インコントロ・データ(P56)

工事種別：ファサードと内装　全面改装
床面積：レストラン370.96㎡(うち厨房84.00㎡)　ホール549.40㎡　合計920.36㎡
工期：1989年７月20日〜10月７日
●営業内容
開店：1989年10月８日
営業時間：午前11時30分〜午後11時
定休日：なし　電話：(03)3708-6161
経営者：日本中央開発㈱
従業員：サービス８人　厨房12人　合計20人

客席数：100席
客単価：6000円　客回転数：約1回
主なメニューと単価：コースメニュー6000～8000　アドリア海風サラダ1800　魚のグリル2600　リゾット(2人前)2000　カルパッチョ3000　魚貝のミックスフライ2400　サラダ各種800　ランチ2000・2500・3000　コーヒー500～600　グラスワイン500　ビール600～700　シェリー700　カクテル800～900
●主な仕上げ材料
サイン：真鍮いぶし仕上げクリア
床：エントランス／臼杵石　レストラン／多胡石　チーク材染色　ホール／ナラフローリングつや消し
壁：エントランス／PB下地AEP塗装　腰壁・ナラ材練り付け　レストラン／PB下地AEP塗装　スタッコ塗り(エポカ／エバーファースト)　ホール／PB下地グラスウールクロス＋ステンレス平織り金網をスチールLアングル枠押さえ　大理石　蛇紋岩　ナラ材練り付けクリア
天井：エントランス&レストラン／PB下地AEP塗装　ホール／グラスウールクロス
照明器具：エントランス／ダウンライト(大光電機)　レストラン／ダウンライト(大光電機)＋スチール製間接照明　ホール／シーリングライト(マックスレイ)
家具：レストラン／椅子・ベンチシート布張り(ペザント／アスワン大装)　ホール／折り畳み椅子(ブリッツ／カッシーナジャパン　ミロ／アイチ)
●撮影：本木誠一('90年3月号)

つかしげ・データ(P59)

工事種別：ファサードと内装　全面改装
床面積：250㎡(うち厨房49㎡)
工期：1990年4月27日～6月17日
総工費：7500万円
解体撤去費150万円　ファサード600万円　サイン50万円　内装造作費2100万円　空調設備費950万円　厨房設備費1000万円　給排水衛生設備費450万円　電気設備費400万円　照明器具費250万円　家具・什器費1000万円　音響設備費50万円　その他(植栽・FRP柱他)500万円
●営業内容
開店：1990年6月7日
営業時間：午前11時～午後9時30分
定休日：日曜日　電話：(06)729-9353
経営者：㈲つかしげ・塚本聿子
従業員：サービス1人　厨房6人　パート・アルバイト常時3人　合計10人
客席数：37席
客単価：1万円　客回転数：1回
主なメニューと単価：昼のコース2500・3500　ディナーコース7000・1万2000(フランス料理)　ビール500　ウイスキー(ロイヤルS)500　グラスワイン500　ワインボトル2600～1万5000
●主な仕上げ材料
外壁：コンクリートブロック＋モルタル下地黒御影石本磨き　せっ器質タイル(フェアストン／名古屋モザイク工業)　白レンガタイル　サッシュ／スチールサッシュレザートーン焼き付け仕上げ　入口扉／天然突き板染色ポリウレタン塗装(タブーシャークウッド／ADコア・ファニイズ・インターナショナル
外部床：粘板岩貼り(ブラックストレート／ABC商会)300角
サイン：鉄板ｔ4.5腐食加工仕上げ
床：モルタル下地砕石樹脂加工床材(ヴァーレストーン／アドヴァン)　一部じゅうたん貼り(ドットウェル)　カウンター部／ブナ材パーケット(パーケ・EZ／ボーゾー)　黒御影石本磨き
幅木：米松染色CLウレタン塗装　H25
壁：PBｔ12下地スタッコ塗装(スタッコアンティコ／エバーファースト)　マツ材杢出しCL(ウエルドウッド／朝日ウッドテック)　アルミサッシュアルマイト仕上げベネチアンガラス嵌め込み(デコラガラス／サカモト)　一部模様吹き付け塗材(ジョリパット／アイカ工業)
天井：PBｔ12下地EPローラー塗装　一部EP多色吹き付け仕上げ
照明器具：ウシオスペックス　遠藤照明
カウンター：甲板／サクラ材染色ポリウレタン塗装
飾り柱：FRP加工
スクリーン：ポリエステルファイバー編み二重がさね
●撮影：柄松　稔('91年1月号)

グルメドーム・データ(P62)

工事種別：一戸建て　新築
用途地域地区：第2種住居専用地域
建ぺい率：制限60%＞実効24.6%
容積率：制限200%＞実効30.7%
構造と規模：S造2階建て　一部木造平屋建て
敷地面積：2166.17㎡　建築面積：532.20㎡
床面積：1階522.54㎡(うち厨房168㎡)　2階142.00㎡　合計664.54㎡
工期：1989年3月14日～7月20日
総工費：1億6000万円
●営業内容
開店：1989年7月26日
営業時間：午前10時～午後11時
定休日：なし　電話：(0723)63-0881
経営者：㈱グルメ杵屋
従業員：サービス2人　厨房4人　パート・アルバイト16人　合計22人
客席数：226席　客単価：1250円
主なメニューと単価：うどん定食590　寿司定食880　ハンバーグ定食690より　和食御膳2400　コーヒー・紅茶290　ビール450
●主な仕上げ材料
屋根：コンパネｔ12アスファルトルーフィング22kg下地亜鉛引鉄板ｔ0.4瓦棒の上に歴青系厚膜タイプ防食塗装(サンシルバー／三晃金属工業)
外壁：ラスモルタル下地アクリルリシン吹き付け
外部床：アスファルト舗装および玉石洗い出し
サイン：スチールおよびアクリルパネル
床：洋食・和イス客席／米松縁甲板ｔ25ワックス仕上げ　和タタミ席／松化粧単板合板フローリングｔ15
壁：PBｔ12下地寒冷紗VP　腰壁(洋食客席)／米松耐水合板(ウエルドパネル／朝日ウッドテック)
天井：洋食客席／マガシロ不燃ピーリング　和イス客席／PBｔ9下地寒冷紗VP　和タタミ客席／杉不燃化粧単板合板底目貼り
●撮影：川元　斉('90年5月号)

オプスおぐに・データ(P66)

工事種別：一戸建て　新築
用途地域地区：指定なし
建ぺい率：実効14.41%　容積率：実効23.27%
構造と規模：RC造およびS造　地上4階建て
敷地面積：5559.18㎡　建築面積：801.18㎡
床面積：レストハウス棟／1階265.05㎡　中2階87.68㎡　2階113.04㎡　3階114.80㎡　4階113.04㎡　小計693.61㎡　ジャクジー棟／102.69㎡　格納庫棟／387.59㎡　機械室棟／110.00㎡　合計1293.89㎡
工期：1991年10月1日～1993年1月12日
総工費：8億8000万円
建築軀体工事費5億7600万円　外構工事費7500万円　サイン800万円　リフト工事費8100万円　駐車場工事費1億400万円　厨房設備費1000万円　家具・什器費2600万円
●営業内容
開店：1993年2月2日
営業時間：午前9時30分～午後10時
定休日：木曜日(1，2，3，5，7，8月を除く)
電話：(0258)95-3161
経営者：㈱小国地域振興公社
主な付帯施設と料金：リフト(1基)／1日券2000円　1回券120円　スノーモビル／初心者体験コース1200円　スクール3500円　レンタル1200～1700円　4輪バギー／レンタル1700円　プール&ジャクジー(7～9月)／大人1300円　子供1000円　ジャクジー(1～6・10～12月)／大人600円　子供400円
〈レストランおよびカフェ〉
従業員：サービス8人　厨房4人　パート・アルバイト常時8人　合計20人
客席数：95席
客単価：レストラン／1000円　カフェ／800円
客回転数：休日3回　平日1回
主なメニューと単価：ボンゴレビアンコ800　ハンバーグステーキ850　ビーフシチュー1200　ビーフカレー700　海老とチキンのドリア1000　コーヒー350　ジュース400　ビール450
●主な仕上げ材料
屋根：外断熱露出アスファルト防水　カラーステンレス防水
外壁：杉板ｔ15縦羽目板貼り木材保護着色塗装(キシラデコール／武田薬品工業)およびオイルステイン　一部コンクリート化粧打ち放し撥水性コンクリート保護材塗布(トップコート／鈴鹿塗料)　杉板ｔ15下見板貼りキシラデコール塗布
外部床：玄昌石貼り　ヒバ材ｔ15融雪パイプ埋め込み
〈ホール〉
床：玄昌石貼り　珪砂敷き
壁：コンクリート打ち放し　暖炉造形／土壁塗り　手すり／スチール錆仕上げCL
天井：PBｔ9下地和紙調ビニルクロス貼り
照明器具：遠藤照明
家具：いづみ木芸　サンセン
〈ジャグジー〉
床：ヒバ材ｔ15貼り　一部玉砂利洗い出し
壁：ヒバ材ｔ15貼り縦羽目板貼り　一部繊維混入石膏板下地(FGボード／浅野スレート)VPユズハダ仕上げ
天井：FGボードｔ8下地VPユズハダ仕上げ
特注家具：アイデック
〈レストラン〉
床：長尺シート模様貼り
壁：FGボードｔ6＋ｔ6下地和紙調ビニルクロス貼り　ケイカル板下地ｔ8＋ｔ8不燃銘木合板貼り　PBｔ9下地和紙調ビニルクロス貼り
特注家具：アイデック
〈カフェ〉
床：長尺シート貼り
壁：FGボードｔ6＋ｔ6下地AEP　一部スチールｔ9SOP
天井：PBｔ9下地AEP
特注家具：アンビエンテ：インターナショナル
●撮影：佐藤振一('93年3月号)

里蘇・データ(P72)

工事種別：ファサードと内装　新築
床面積：218㎡(うち厨房48㎡)
工期：1992年11月13日～12月25日
●営業内容
開店：1993年1月27日
営業時間：午前10時～午後10時
定休日：水曜日(ハイシーズンは無休)
経営者：ラクス㈱　電話：(0557)51-4846
従業員：サービス3人　厨房3人　合計6人
客席数：85席　客回転数：2回
客単価：昼／1000円　夜／1500円
主なメニューと単価：吹き寄せ風天麩羅の御飯1500　駿河湾鮮魚の洋風ちらし1800　渡り蟹のブルターニュ風1800　ビール650　コーヒー・紅茶500
●主な仕上げ材料
床：コンパネｔ12二重貼り下地マホガニー寄せ木貼り(メッセージフロア／朝日ウッドテック)
壁：軽鉄組みPBｔ12下地アクリル系吹き付け塗材(ラフトン／鈴鹿塗料)　一部寒冷紗パテシゴキ塩ビシート貼り(ダイノックシート／住友スリーエム)　目地・押さえ縁／タモ材染色ウレタンクリア塗装
天井：軽鉄組みPBｔ12下地寒冷紗パテシゴキEP
照明：波形光天井／アクリルｔ3布貼り曲面加工　アッパー照明／アクリルｔ10フロスト加工　スタンド照明／フロスト加工　支柱・スチールφ15メタリック塗装
家具：バーカウンター／甲板・シカモア染色ウレタンクリア塗装　レジカウンター／人工大理石(コーリアン／ABC商会)　テーブル／甲板・シカモア材突き板(フレスコ／ADコア)
●撮影：野口　毅('93年7月号)

作品データ

ビア&ステーキレストラン

クリスタルコート・データ(P76)

工事種別：内装のみ　新築
床面積：617.3㎡(うち厨房45.7㎡)
工期：1990年8月1日～9月30日
●営業内容
開店：1990年11月2日
営業時間：午前11時～午後11時　定休日：なし
電話：(06)949-5255　経営者：丸和観光㈱
従業員：サービス10人　厨房10人　パート・アルバイト常時50人　合計70人
客席数：233席　客回転数：3回
客単価：昼間1000円　夜間2800円
主なメニューと単価：前菜の盛り合せ1400　ポテトの香味焼イタリア風600　サラダ500～1200　イカとエビの地中海フライ1200　スープ500～1000　鴨ロースバター焼1200　特製ビーフシチュー1200　アドリブビール・一番搾り・クリスタルラガー500
●主な仕上げ材料
サイン：ステンレス鏡面仕上げ切り文字
床：貝殻入り樹脂加工タイル(ヴァーレストーン／アドヴァン)　粘板岩タイル(ファーバン／アドヴァン)　大理石パターン貼り　割りガラスタイル埋め込みモルタルウレタン塗装　タイルパターン貼り　ナラ材フローリングW200染色ウレタン仕上げ
壁：PBｔ9下地模様吹き付け塗材(ジョリパット／アイカ工業)　擬石貼り(カルチャーストーン／トコナメ)
柱：ゴールドタイル貼り(ハイメタル／淡陶)カルチャーストーン貼り
スクリーン飾り柱：FRP大谷石塗装(ボーマン美術装飾)
天井：RC打ち放し　鉄筋吊り天井錆仕上げ　一部カーテン取り付け
照明器具：カウンター特注ペンダント(松下電工)
カウンター：ナラ材&メープル材染色ウレタン仕上げモザイク貼り　一部ガラスタイル埋め込み
家具：イス・テーブル／アスプルンド(島本)
●撮影：山田誠良('91年1月号)

クイクイ・データ(P80)

工事種別：ファサードと内装　新築
床面積：1311.56㎡(うち厨房259.37㎡)
工期：1992年6月1日～9月10日
●営業内容
開店：1992年10月1日
営業時間：午前11時～午後11時　定休日：なし
電話：(078)360-0808
経営者：キリンビール㈱　運営：㈱はや
従業員：サービス6人　厨房5人　パート・アルバイト常時149人　合計160人
客席数：500席
客単価：2300円　客回転数：4回
主なメニューと単価：牛肉のカルパッチョ700　クイクイ風ドネルケバブのプレート1300　手作りジャンボコロッケ神戸風650　ドラフトビール(ジョッキ)500・650
●主な仕上げ材料
外壁：ケイカル板下地御影石貼り(グラナイトキャステルロック／エイベック)
外部床：モルタル下地ビニル床タイル貼り(シャール／エルエスアイ)
床：モルタル下地石英砂入り塗り床仕上げ(リバーストーンカーペット／アドヴァン)　コンクリート洗い出しクラック入り　ビニル床タイル乱貼り(ユーロマーブル／エルエスアイ)　砂固めステンレス&ガラスチップ入り　通路／コンクリート洗い出しR目地真鍮埋め込み　一部モザイクタイル貼り(エバーファースト)
壁：PBｔ12下地シックイ汚し仕上げ　ナラ材染色CL　一部石貼り(リバーロックセラブリック／エイベック)
天井：PBｔ12下地AEP　モザイクタイル貼り　ナラ材パターン貼り
照明器具：吊り下げ照明(アート・デ・メキシロ)
家具：椅子(キノシタ，小泉産業，ボスミック，コスガ)　カウンター／ナラ材染色ウレタン仕上げ　石貼り　籐アジロ組み　漆　スチール磨き仕上げ
什器：マーケット台／ナラ荒木染色CL飾りビス止め
●撮影：柄松　稔('93年1月号)

心斎橋倶楽部・データ(P84)

工事種別：内装のみ　全面改装
床面積：633.9㎡(うち厨房125.4㎡)
工期：1992年11月10日～12月17日
●営業内容
開店日：1992年12月18日
営業時間：午後5時～午前0時　定休日：なし
電話：(06)213-1098　経営者：延田興業㈱
従業員：サービス5人　厨房7人　パート・アルバイト常時20人　合計32人
客席数：380席
客単価：3100円　客回転数：1.2回
主なメニューと単価：モウモウサラダメキシコ編500　心斎橋倶楽部推薦ビーフストロガノフ800　牛鍋3800　心斎橋倶楽部特製でっかいパフェ950　鶴橋のブタキムチ500　もちもちグラタン500　ビール中ジョッキ550　カクテル600　ソフトドリンク類500　エビアン200
●主な仕上げ材料
床：コンクリート下地モルタル木ゴテ押さえ　一部ナチ石埋め込み
壁：PBｔ20およびモルタル＋下地調整材(スーパーエスモルジョイントV／日丸産業)の上カラープラスターサンダー仕上げ
天井：梁／松丸太皮剝き
照明器具：ハロゲン　一部ロサンゼルス直輸入
●撮影：柄松　稔('93年12月号)

フラムドール・データ(P88)

工事種別：内装のみ　新築
床面積：1階526.41㎡　2階494.73㎡　合計1021.14㎡
工期：1988年7月8日～1989年10月31日
●営業内容
開店：1989年11月28日
営業時間：午前11時30分～午後10時
定休日：なし　電話：(03)5608-5381
経営者：㈱ニューアサヒ
従業員：サービス30人　厨房30人　合計60人
客席数：1階120席　2階120席　合計240席
客単価：4000円　客回転数：1.5回
主なメニューと単価：オードブル1200～3200　魚料理1800～2400　肉料理2100～3600　サラダ1200　チーズ1400　赤ワイン3000～7500　白ワイン2400～7000　スーパードライ生ビール330㎖350　500㎖550　1800㎖1600　酒600
●主な仕上げ材料
屋根：アスファルト防水の上軽量コンクリート金ゴテ押さえ
外壁：黒御影石(ジンバブエ)本磨き打ち込みPC版　アルミキャスト製丸窓(特注品)
外部床：中国産サクラ御影石割り肌仕上げ　磁器質タイル貼り200角(ピアッツア／イナックス)　歩行用ガラスブロック300角照明内蔵
屋上オブジェ：スチール外殻構造フッ素樹脂塗装
床：白大理石(タソスホワイト)貼り水磨き仕上げ600角　鉛板貼りｔ5
幅木：鉛シート貼り　H1200
壁：ベルベットフトン張り　一部白大理石(タソスホワイト)ショットブラスト仕上げ　柱／トラスウォール下地プラスター塗り
天井：軽鉄組み繊維強化石膏ボード(FGボード／浅野スレート)下地スウェード調吹き付け塗装(フェロックストーン／グレー／藤倉化成)FGボード下地EP(白)
照明器具：ローボルトハロゲン12V(特注品)
●撮影：ナカサ&パートナーズ('90年1月号)

しゃぶ鮮・データ(P92)

工事種別：ファサードと内装　新築
床面積：413.45㎡(うち厨房102.06㎡)
工期：1991年7月1日～8月31日
総工費：2億380万円
●営業内容
開店：1991年10月1日
営業時間：平日／午後4時～午後11時　日曜・祭日／午後3時～午後10時
定休日：第3月曜日　電話：(0422)48-0141
経営者：㈱アバウト　星　和夫
従業員：サービス3人　厨房2人　パート・アルバイト常時20人　合計25人
客席数：140席
客単価：3800円　客回転数：0.8回
主なメニューと単価：しゃぶしゃぶコース2500　3500　ケサリーヤ750　トルティーヤ・バラエティー1200　しゃぶしゃぶサラダ800　紙包み焼き1000　生ビール650　黒生ビール700　ハーフ&ハーフ700　ワイン(グラス)500，(デカンタ)1200　オレンジジュース500　コーヒー400
●主な仕上げ材料
サイン：真鍮箱文字(バックライト)
床：樹脂系タイルパターン貼り(アロマナチュール／アドヴァン)　タガヤサンムク材フローリング
幅木：モルタル金ゴテAEP
壁：PBｔ12下地AEP　一部特注スチール貼り錆仕上げ　パーティション／特注スチール錆仕上げ　透明ガラス嵌め込みｔ5　一部鏡貼り
天井：スケルトン　吊り天井／スチール製NECO写真貼り
照明器具：スポットライト(ウシオスペックス)
家具：特注椅子，ガスコンロ組み込み特注テーブル，電磁調理器組み込み特注テーブル(ガウディートランス)
什器：特注サービスキャビネット(ガウディートランス)
●撮影：野口　毅('92年5月号)

キリン万代橋ホール・データ(P95)

工事種別：ファサードと内装　全面改装
構造と規模：RC造　地上4階建て(うち店舗は1・2階)
敷地面積：345㎡
床面積：1階304㎡(うち厨房82㎡)　2階82㎡(うち厨房22㎡)　合計386㎡(うち厨房104㎡)
工期：1991年8月25日～11月21日
総工費：1億4000万円
●営業内容
開店：1991年11月28日
営業時間：午後5時～午後11時
定休日：なし　電話：(025)246-7777
経営者：㈱キリン万代橋ホール
従業員：サービス5人　厨房5人　パート・アルバイト常時12人　合計22人
客席数：230席
客単価：3000円　客回転数：1.5回
主なメニューと単価：あさりの中国酒風味800　蒸籠(せいろ)蒸し480～550　ピロシキ470　焼肉670　ビーフストロガノフ1100　ケジャン1800　生ビール／大800　中600　ピッチャー2100　ワイン／グラス450　ボトル2500　地酒720，930
●主な仕上げ材料
外壁：既存コンクリートEP　サッシ／アルミサッシOP
サイン：真鍮切り文字
床：1階／タイル貼り300角　2階／フローリング染色仕上げW100
幅木：スプルスCL
壁・天井：1階／リシン吹き付け下地EP吹き付け　2階／PBｔ12下地クロス貼りAEPローラー仕上げ　一部アルミ目地　スプルスCL見切り材　天井格子／スプルス角材組み60角飾り真鍮棒
照明器具：特注造作(スポットライト，DLを除く)
家具・什器：スプルスおよびアガチス材クリアウレタン
●撮影：ナカサ&パートナーズ('92年2月号)

ビアマーケット西院・データ(P98)

協力：照明(波紋のライティング)／高橋洋子　ロゴデザイン，屏風絵／上田ミユキ　グラフィックデザイン／デーゲー　野本卓司　スタイリング，アプリケーション／AFA　真砂三千代
工事種別：内装のみ　新築
床面積：370㎡(うち厨房115㎡)
工期：1992年6月15日～8月10日
総工費：1億2560万円
●営業内容
開店：1992年10月1日
営業時間：平日／午前11時30分～午後2時30分　午後5時～午後11時　日曜・祭日／午前11時30分～午後11時
定休日：なし　電話：(075)316-1233
経営者：㈱スター食堂
従業員：サービス4人　厨房4人　パート・アルバイト常時21人　合計29人
客席数：154席　客単価：昼1200円　夜3000円
客回転数：1.4回
主なメニューと単価：鍋物各種(1人前)2500～5000　肉料理550～980　点心各種400　サラダ600～800　ビール450・530　冷酒1200
●主な仕上げ材料

床：コンクリート金ゴテ下地防塵塗装　コンパネt12下地ナラフローリング貼り木材保護着色塗装　フレキシブルボードt8ウレタン塗装
壁：CB化粧積みモルタル薄塗り　モルタル下地和紙貼り
天井：LGS組みフレキシブルボードt6
●撮影：藤原　弘('93年1月号)

キリンの館・データ(P101)

工事種別：ファサードと内装　新築
床面積：135.0㎡(うち厨房20.9㎡)
工期：1990年2月9日～3月10日
総工費：5400万円
●営業内容
開店：1990年3月20日
営業時間：午前11時～午後11時
定休日：第3水曜日　電話：(06)354-6888
経営者：㈱千隆
従業員：サービス1人　厨房2人　パート・アルバイト常時10人　合計13人
客席数：80席
客単価：2000円　客回転数：2.5回
主なメニューと単価：スペアリブ980　カーニバルサラダ500　貝柱のバター焼きニンニクしょう油650　キムチと豚肉いため550　生ビール(グラス) 400　生ビール(大ピッチャー) 1600
●主な仕上げ材料
外壁：有孔耐火ボード下地しっくい塗り　クリアガラスt10　FBt9×100フェノール樹脂系塗装(カンペフェロドール／関西ペイント)
サイン：アルミ板t5　シルク印刷
床：モルタル金ゴテ深草石埋め込み　目地／ステンレス　ナラフローリング貼りt15
壁：軽鉄組みPBt12下地寒冷紗パテシゴキAEPローラーおよびラッカー吹き付け
天井：軽鉄組みPBt12下地寒冷紗AEPローラー　一部アルミパンチング板t1.5　既存スラブAEP吹き付け
椅子：スチールメラミン焼き付け　座／シナ合板ウレタン塗装　サイドチェア(ADコア・ファニイズ・インターナショナル)
テーブル：ナラ材ウレタン塗装
カウンター：トップ／ブビンガ・ナラウレタン塗装　ステンレスHL　アルミ板貼り分け
●撮影：名執一雄('91年1月号)

海鮮麦酒屋・データ(P104)

工事種別：ファサードと内装　新築
床面積：レストラン274.7㎡(うち厨房67.5㎡)　バー36.9㎡(うち厨房18.0㎡)　合計311.6㎡
工期：1990年1月20日～4月30日
総工費：1億3000万円
ファサード費800万円　サイン100万円　内装造作費4500万円　空調設備費1200万円　厨房設備費1000万円　給排水衛生設備費700万円　電気設備費800万円　照明器具費600万円　家具・什器費1500万円　音響設備費600万円　オブジェ製作費1200万円
●営業内容
開店：1990年5月10日
営業時間：午前8時～午後11時
定休日：日曜・祭日・第三土曜日
電話：(06)262-5159　経営者：河野殖産㈱
従業員：サービス3人　厨房6人　パート・アルバイト常時15人　合計24人
客席数：レストラン96席 バー30席 合計126席
客単価：レストラン3500円　バー2500円
客回転数：2.5回(レストランのみ)
主なメニューと単価：麦酒屋のおよぎ魚(平目) 6800円　牛肉のたたき900　甘海老の唐揚700　兜煮1200　海草サラダ600　海鮮てんぷら盛り1500　海鮮雑炊1000　ドラフトビール400　一番搾り550　ウイスキーS600～900　日本酒(一合)500～700
●主な仕上げ材料
サイン：タモ材脱色ウレタン塗装　板面／鉄板腐食加工　文字／ステンレス鏡面
床：レストラン／モルタル下地テラゾタイル(ヴィアーレ／フッコー)　玉砂利洗い出し那知石ステンレスチップ入り　バー／ナラ材フローリングW180乱貼り　座敷／琉球オモテ畳へりなし
幅木：モルタル刷毛引き仕上H300
壁：レストラン&バー／軽量鉄骨組みラスボード下地プラスター刷毛引き仕上げ　座敷／プラスター中塗りカラーしっくい仕上げ　下部鉄板錆加工
飾り柱：タモ材脱色90角　下部鉄板錆加工
天井：既存RCスラブVP　アルミパンチングプレート吊り下げ　スチールルーバーちぢみ塗装　ステンレス鏡面仕上げ　一部石吊り
照明器具：小泉産業　松下電工
家具：インターデコール　アンビエンテ・インターナショナル　ADコア・ファニイズ・インターナショナル
スクリーン：フレーム／異形鉄筋シャフト錆加工　真鍮板取り付けφ900
カウンター：甲板／タモ材脱色ウレタン仕上げ　腰／タモ集成材脱色ウレタン仕上げ
テーブル：甲板／メープル材染色クリアウレタン仕上げ　脚／スチール角パイプ黒ちぢみ塗装
●撮影：福本正明('91年2月号)

キャフェ ボーミエ・データ(P107)

工事種別：ファサードと内装　新築
床面積：1・2階各95.20㎡(うち厨房34.91㎡)　合計190.40㎡
工期：1993年4月8日～7月12日
●営業内容
開店：1993年7月19日
営業時間：午前9時～午後10時
定休日：土曜・日曜・祭日
電話：(03)5466-2242
経営者：東建インターナショナル㈱
従業員：サービス1人　厨房2人　パート・アルバイト常時5人　合計8人
客席数：1階27席　2階37席　合計64席
客単価：ランチ700円　夜2500円
主なメニューと単価：ランチ750　700　680　牛ヒレ肉しょうゆマスタード焼き600　ポテトグラタンアイダホ風450　チキンソテーインド風煮込み500　ケーキ400～500　コーヒー400　紅茶450　ビール400　水割り350
●主な仕上げ材料
外壁：アルミカーテンウォール陽極酸化被膜2種　熱線吸収ガラス　一部熱線吸収反射ガラス　RC打ち放し　フッ素樹脂系吹き付けタイル
外部床：磁器質タイル貼り150角
サイン：ステンレス焼き付け塗装特殊ムラ着色
床：塩ビタイルシート貼り　特注カーペット貼り(ニッケ)　カーペットおさえ／特注金物(アインズ)　ナラ材フローリング直貼り　一部特注カーペット敷き(ニッケ)
幅木：ナラ材　H100
壁：軽鉄組みPBt9+t12下地砕石混入スタッコ金ゴテ仕上げ　窓台／スチール鋼板t1.6水溶性ツヤありエマルション系塗材　腰壁／軽鉄組みPBt9+t12下地水溶性ツヤありエマルション系塗材　手摺り・ドレープ金物／アイアン特注金物(アインズ)
天井：軽鉄組みPBt9+t12下地クロス貼り
照明器具：松下電工　東芝
特注家具：アルベロ・ベルトイア　イデー
什器：カウンター／合板下地ポリパテ荒らしの上研磨　ポリウレタンクリア着色+乳白ポリカーボネート板貼り
ドレープ：布+ハトメφ40ブラス色
●撮影：ナカサ&パートナーズ('93年12月号)

つぼハ ペンギンズ スクエア店・データ(P110)

工事種別：ファサードと内装　新築
床面積：地下2階352.01㎡(うち厨房59㎡)　地下1階269.26㎡(うち厨房20.5㎡)　中地下1階38.41㎡　合計659.68㎡(うち厨房79.5㎡)
工期：1992年9月10日～11月25日
●営業内容
開店：1992年11月30日
営業時間：午後5時～午前0時　定休日：なし
電話：(06)312-4567
経営者：㈲ペンギンズバー　望月達朗
従業員：サービス3人　厨房4人　パート・アルバイト常時40人　合計47人
客席数：300席
客単価：2000円　客回転数：1.2回
主なメニューと単価：肉料理360～　魚料理300～　ポテト料理300～　揚げ物380～　サラダ360～　もつ鍋430　焼きおにぎり170　ビール430　サワー280　酒240～
●主な仕上げ材料
床：システムフロア下地杉板t36TS拭き取りワックス仕上げ　モルタル下地モザイクタイルパターン貼り　チェッカードプレートCL仕上げ
幅木：トラバーチン本磨き　H120
壁：ラスボード下地プラスターこて押さえ　鉄骨組み　複合板下地白砂岩乱貼り　目地／プラスター
天井：ラスボード下地プラスターこて押さえ　既存キーストンプレート吹き付け塗装
●撮影：松村芳治('92年5月号)

ビアクリスタル・データ(P114)

工事種別：内装のみ　新築
床面積：806.68㎡(うち厨房194.28㎡)
工期：1992年6月1日～9月20日
●営業内容
開店：1992年10月1日
営業時間：午前11時～午後10時
定休日：なし　電話：(078)360-6052
経営者：ビアクリスタル㈱
従業員：サービス5人　厨房7人　パート・アルバイト常時23人　合計35人
客席数：219席
客単価：2800円　客回転数：1.6回
主なメニューと単価：おすすめ日替わりランチ800　テンダーロインステーキ(200g)2400　ビーフステーキとロブスター4000　ディナーセット・テンダーロインコース4500　ソフトドリンク400
●主な仕上げ材料
床：モルタル下地蛇紋石・黒御影石本磨き貼り分けt15　アルミおよびスチールチェッカードプレートt6　タイルカーペット貼り(アスワン)　ステンレス，真鍮目地棒
壁：PBt12下地アルミおよびスチールチェッカードプレートt6貼り　黒皮鉄板一部錆仕上げ　亜鉛鉄板　真鍮板ハンマートーン仕上げ
天井：ステンレスメッシュt2三重張り　PBt12下地ラッカー吹き付け塗装　小波スレート　コンクリート用塗膜防水材仕上げ　スチールチェッカードプレートt3　真鍮板古色仕上げ
照明器具：ハロゲンランプ(小泉産業)
家具：椅子(ラグーザ／相合家具製作所)
●撮影：柄松　稔('93年1月号)

アルテミス・データ(P118)

工事種別：内装のみ　新築
床面積：157.39㎡(厨房97.93㎡，ホテル厨房と兼用，床面積には含まず)
工期：1989年9月25日～11月18日
●営業内容
開店：1989年11月24日
営業時間：午前7時～午前10時　午前11時30分～午後2時　午後5時30分～午後10時
定休日：なし　電話：(06)446-6111
経営者：河野殖産㈱
従業員：サービス2人　厨房6人　パート・アルバイト常時2人　合計10人
客席数：60席
客単価：5000～7000円　客回転数：3回
主なメニューと単価：シーフードランチ1500～3000　シーフードコース5000・7000・1万　ステーキランチ2500～4000　ステーキコース8000・1万・1万3000　ビール600　ホテルワイン(ボトル)3500　(グラス)600　シャブリ9000　コーヒー・紅茶各500
●主な仕上げ材料
床：モルタル下地カーペット敷き(ニューマイク／川島織物)　塩ビタイル貼り(グラニットタイル／シンコール)　ビニルチップ複層塗材(コルトラモザイク／エバーファースト)
幅木：オーク材染色CL　H40
壁：PBt12下地スタッコ金ゴテ仕上げ(スタッコ・アンティコ／エバーファースト)　柱形／石膏鋳型ドレープ仕上げ
天井：PBt12下地クロス貼りAEP(タッソー／川島織物)　格子天井／シナ合板フラッシュt60AEP
照明器具：スクリーンスタンド合成綿布特注品　照明内蔵　柱上部飾り照明／FRP成形特注品
家具・什器：テーブル／スタッコ・アンティコの上にウレタン磨き仕上げ　イス／メープル染色ウレタンクリア仕上げ　鉄板焼カウンター天板／外国産花崗岩　腰／ナラ材染色ウレタンクリア仕上げ　ドアハンドル／真鍮鋳物成形青銅色仕上げ(ユニオン装飾金物)
●撮影：福本正明('90年4月号)

ステーキジロー・データ(P121)

工事種別：一戸建て　新築
用途地域地区：市街化調整区域
建ぺい率：制限70%>実効35%
容積率：制限400%>実効65%
構造と規模：S造　地上2階建て
敷地面積：839㎡　建築面積：293㎡

作品データ

床面積：１階258㎡　２階293㎡(うち厨房40㎡)合計551㎡
工期：1989年11月１日〜1990年８月４日
●営業内容
開店：1990年８月５日
営業時間：午前11時〜午後11時
定休日：なし　電話：(0942)45-1111
経営者：㈱リューカ　中村善立
従業員：サービス１人　厨房３人　パート・アルバイト常時３人　合計７人
客席数：60席
客単価：3000円　客回転数：1.5回
主なメニューと単価：和牛ステーキセット5500　ステーキランチ1500　季節のディナー--3800
●主な仕上げ材料
屋根：木毛板下地ステンレス板葺き
外壁：押し出し成形セメント板貼り(ラムダサイディング／昭和電工建材)　一部特殊樹脂モルタル塗り　火山岩貼り
床：コンクリート下地フローリング貼り　粘板岩貼り(マジスタスレート／アドヴァン)
壁：ＰＢｔ12寒冷紗パテ下地ＡＥＰ　柱・梁／特殊樹脂モルタル塗り
天井：強化石膏板ｔ８寒冷紗パテ下地ＡＥＰ
●撮影：明倫館('93年８月号)

いわい・データ(Ｐ124)

工事種別：内装のみ　新築
床面積：181.76㎡(うち厨房22.59㎡)
工期：1988年10月１日〜12月23日
総工費：8250万円
解体撤去費30万円　サイン50万円　内装造作費3800万円　空調設備費550万円　厨房設備費600万円　給排水衛生設備費570万円　電気設備費550万円　照明器具費250万円　家具・什器費900万円　音響設備費50万円　ステーキカウンター(甲板は含まず)900万円
●営業内容
開店：1988年12月24日
営業時間：午前11時30分〜午後３時　午後５時〜午後11時
定休日：月曜日　電話：(0427)22-4847
経営者：㈲岩井商事
従業員：サービス４人　厨房４人　パート・アルバイト常時１人　合計９人
客席数：57席　客回転数：約２回
客単価：昼3500円　夜１万5000円
主なメニューと単価：コースメニューのみ
昼／フランス料理2500・5000　夜／すてーき会席5000・7000・１万　ビール700　ハウスワイン(ハーフ)800　(グラス)600　ワイン／シャブリ9000　シャトーラフルール１万
●主な仕上げ材料
外壁：客席開口部／アンティークエッチンググラス扉　アンティークステンドグラス　エントランス／古レンガ積み
サイン：古材くり抜き
床：風除室／古レンガ敷き込み　客席／コンパネｔ12下地チークフローリング乱尺貼りおよびチーク寄せ木貼り(ダイヤブロック／ミハマ)　ステーキカウンター内／コンパネｔ12下地リノリウム貼り(ロンリウム／ロンシール工業)
幅木：通路／古レンガ積み　H300　客席／大理石本磨きH300　木製見切りH200　パーティールーム／アンティーク陶板H300　木製見切りH200
壁：風除室&バー／古レンガ積み　客席&通路／プラスター金ゴテ仕上げ　一部レザー貼り
天井：ラスボードｔ７下地プラスター金ゴテ押さえ　梁／けやき古材
家具：イス／ヴィットマンおよびトーネット(アイデック)　隅棚／松本民芸家具
●撮影：鳴瀬　亨('90年４月号)

オクスン 北方・データ(Ｐ127)

工事種別：一戸建て　新築
用途地域地区：第２種住居専用地域
建ぺい率：制限70%＞実効29.7%
容積率：制限200%＞実効38.0%
構造と規模：Ｓ造　地上２階建て
敷地面積：537.91㎡　建築面積：159.75㎡
床面積：１階159.75㎡(うち厨房38.25㎡)　２階(事務室等)47.25 ㎡　合計207.00㎡
工期：1989年７月26日〜11月20日
総工費：5950万円
建築軀体工事費2280万円　外構工事費100万円　サイン80万円　内装造作費860万円　空調設備費340万円　厨房設備費567万円　給排水衛生設備費1000万円　電気設備費145万円　照明器具費126万円　家具・什器費410万円　音響設備費42万円
●営業内容
開店：1989年12月１日
営業時間：午前11時30分〜午後２時　午後５時30分〜午後10時
定休日：火曜日　電話(0583)23-0390
経営者：Ｉ.Ｆ.Ｃ.今井食品㈱　今井　昇
従業員：サービス６人　厨房２人　パート・アルバイト常時１人　合計９人
客席数：41席　客単価：3000〜4000円
客回転数：1.5〜２回
主なメニューと単価：オクスンコース5800　飛騨牛コース8800　しゃぶしゃぶコース3500　サーロインコース3950　シーフードコース3000　ヤングコース2500　ビール600　コーヒー500　ワイン(ボトル)2100〜6500　ウイスキー(ボトル)3200・5000
●主な仕上げ材料
屋根：耐水合板ｔ12下地　カラー鉄板瓦棒葺き　一部平葺き
外壁：珪酸カルシウム板ｔ10目透かし貼り下地模様吹き付け塗材(ジョリパット／アイカ工業)　腰壁／角波カラー鉄板貼り(淀川製鋼所)
外部床：土間コンクリート下地ブラックスレート板貼り(ＡＢＣ商会)　一部タイル貼り
床：土間コンクリート下地フローリング貼り　ブラックスレート貼り
壁：ＰＢｔ12下地ビニルクロス貼り(名古屋吉村)　石チップ混入モルタル掻き落とし　柱形／ナラ合板およびシナ合板着色ウレタンクリア塗装
天井：ＰＢｔ12下地ビニルクロス貼り　吊り天井／ナラ合板目透かし貼り着色ウレタン塗装
照明器具：ダウンライト　スポットライト(マックスレイ)
家具：ナラ練り付け合板およびスプルス練り付け合板着色ウレタンクリア塗装
●撮影：加斗タカオ('90年６月号)

楽亭・データ(Ｐ130)

工事種別：内装のみ　新築
床面積：79.5㎡(うち厨房16.7㎡／オープンキッチン含む)
工期：1989年12月10日〜1990年１月15日
総工費：3600万円
●営業内容
開店：1990年２月25日
営業時間：午前11時30分〜午後２時30分　午後５時〜午後10時30分
定休日：火曜日　電話：(03)3623-1220
経営者：㈲喜家
従業員：サービス５人　厨房３人　パート・アルバイト常時３人　合計11人
客席数：48席　客単価：昼2000円　夜6000円
主なメニューと単価：ランチ1200　1500　2000　遊懐石コース3500　楽懐石コース5500　洋風しゃぶしゃぶコース5500　山形牛ステーキコース6500　山形地酒600〜800　山形ワイン／グラス500　ボトル3500
●主な仕上げ材料
床：ナラ材ＯＳＣＬ　琉球畳　石英岩(クォーツサイト／アドヴァン)
幅木：モルタル目地切りＯＳＣＬ
壁：モルタル金ゴテＯＳＣＬ
柱形：大谷石貼り
天井：コンクリート打ち放しＶＰ　吊り天井／タモ材木組みＥＰ　タモ合板ＶＰ小型ＤＬ内蔵　カウンター天蓋／タモ材木組みＥＰ
照明器具：スポットライト　入り口／アンティークランプ
ディスプレイ棚：大谷石積み　透明ガラスｔ８
カウンター天板：ブビンガ材ムク
●撮影：鈴木　光('90年５月号)

石土炉・データ(Ｐ132)

工事種別：内装のみ　新築
床面積：141.13㎡(うち厨房17.32㎡)
工期：1990年12月初旬〜1991年１月下旬
●営業内容
開店：1991年２月14日
営業時間：午前11時30分〜午後３時　午後５時〜午後11時
定休日：なし　電話：(03)3296-1406
経営者：㈱メゾン・ド・フランス
従業員：サービス１人　厨房１人　パート・アルバイト常時８人　合計10人
客席数：60席　客単価：6500円
主なメニューと単価：石焼コース4800・6800　石焼牛コース1200・1800　石鍋しゃぶしゃぶコース4800・6800　石鍋牛ロース1000・1600　サーロインステーキ2000　ワイン3000・4800・7000　グラスワイン500　生ビール500　日本酒600
●主な仕上げ材料
床：モルタル下地粘板岩貼り400角(インターレート／フッコー)　本畳敷きｔ60
壁：腰／石灰岩貼り400×200(ライムストーン／フッコー)　ラスボードｔプラスター塗り下地しっくい金ゴテ押さえ&化学リシン木ゴテ押さえ(マヂックコート／フッコー)
天井：ＰＢｔ９下地寒冷紗貼りＡＥＰ
照明器具：大光電機　ヤマギワ
テーブル：タモ化粧合板ｔ６染色塗装
椅子：モニック
飾り棚：米松ｔ90生地仕上げ
●撮影：鳴瀬　亨('91年12月号)

カフェ&ファストフード

ゼクウ・データ(Ｐ136)

工事種別：ファサードと内装　全面改装
床面積：地下１階72.05㎡(うち厨房10.17㎡)　１階80.95㎡(うち厨房10.66㎡)　２階78.07㎡(うち厨房12.88㎡)　３階81.00㎡(うち厨房30.89㎡)　合計312.07㎡(うち厨房64.60㎡)
工期：1990年９月１日〜11月31日
●営業内容
開店：1990年12月３日
営業時間：午前11時30分〜午後11時
定休日：月１回　電話：(03)3535-5030
経営者：㈱ウメザワ
従業員：サービス２人　厨房１人　パート・アルバイト常時12人　合計15人
客席数：地下１階36席　１階33席　２階38席　３階30席（着席の場合）　合計137席
客単価：昼1000円　夜3000円
主なメニューと単価：ランチ(午前11時30分〜５時)タラコスパゲティ1200　シーフードスパゲティ1200　ビーフライス1300(以上サラダ，コーヒー付)　午後５時以降／前菜盛り合わせ1800　牛タンの塩焼950　カニ爪のフライ900　牛肉のオーブン焼き1300　ブレンドコーヒー550　紅茶600　ビール600　ハウスワイン／グラス2600　ボトル4500　ウイスキー／Ｓ600　Ｗ1000　ボトル7000
●主な仕上げ材料
ファサード：鍛造鉄特殊塗装
床：モルタル下地カリン材フローリング　地下１階／豆砂利コテ押さえ(ミュールコート／旭化成工業)
壁：軽鉄組みラスボードｔ７下地シックイ塗り
天井：軽鉄組みラスボードｔ７下地シックイ塗り　１階天蓋／クルミ　カツラ　支柱・鍛造鉄
家具：アメリカンブラックウォルナット　クルミ　チーク(製作／108)
●撮影：野口　毅('91年２月号)

オリエンタルウェーブ&ラジーニ・データ(Ｐ140)

工事種別：ファサードと内装　全面改装
床面積：１階357㎡(うち厨房23㎡)　２階280㎡(うち厨房26㎡)　合計637㎡
工期：1992年12月１日〜1993年３月31日
●営業内容
〈カフェ オリエンタルウェーブ〉
開店：1993年４月12日
定休日：なし　営業時間：午前11時〜午後11時
電話：(03)3203-2881　経営者：中台工業㈱
従業員：サービス２人　厨房１人　パート・アルバイト常時５人　合計８人
客席数：61席　客単価：900円
客回転数：平日／４回　土・日・祭日／５回
主なメニューと単価：タピオカのプディング700　花巻400〜700　オリエンタルティー800　ロイヤルミルクティー700　マスカットティー700
〈ラジーニ〉
開店：1991年４月12日　定休日：なし
営業時間：午後５時〜午前０時
電話(03)3203-2878　経営者：中台工業㈱
従業員：サービス３人　厨房４人　パート・アルバイト常時７人　合計14人
客席数：74席
客単価：3500円　客回転数：１回
主なメニューと単価：北インドカレー750　ビ

ール600　ウイスキー600～3000
●主な仕上げ材料
外壁：御影石貼り（ピンクポリーノ）本磨きおよびジェットバーナー仕上げ
外部床：御影石貼り（ピンクポリーノ）ジェットバーナー仕上げ
サイン：真鍮ミガキ＋ネオン管
床：大理石貼り（クレママーフィル　セベポロイヤル蛇紋）本磨き　メイプル材フローリング
幅木：木製SOP塗装　H150，120
壁：PBt９＋t12下地AEP塗装　アルミ焼き付け塗装板ガラスt６はめ込み　柱・パーティション／バーズアイメープル染色CL
天井：PBt９＋t12下地AEP塗装
カウンター：メイプル材染色ウレタン塗装
●撮影：ナカサ＆パートナーズ（'93年７月号）

ザ ビッグ ライフ・データ（P144）

工事種別：ファサードと内装　新築
床面積：2534㎡（うち厨房346㎡）
工期：1992年９月21日～1993年３月31日
●営業内容
開店：1993年４月２日
営業時間：午前11時～午後11時
定休日：なし　電話：（092）847-1547
経営者：㈱ツインドームシティ
従業員：サービス11人　厨房12人　パート・アルバイト常時127人　合計150人
客席数：1000席
客単価：2700円　客回転数：1.2回
主なメニューと単価：ピザ・アウトフィールド800　ホール・オブ・フェイムバーガー700　バロン・オブ・ビーフ・サンドイッチ800　生ビール500　フローズンカクテル700　ウイスキー400～
●主な仕上げ材料
入り口オブジェ：鉄骨組みアルミ板貼りt３
床：コンクリート下地ウレタンクリア　ナラ材染色フローリング
壁：軽鉄組みPBt12下地EP三分ツヤ
天井：軽鉄組みPBt12下地EPツヤ消し
●撮影：ナカサ＆パートナーズ（'93年５月号）

原宿フープタウン・データ（P148）

工事種別：一戸建て　新築
用途地域地区：商業地域　住居地域
建ぺい率：制限98.97％＞実効55.50％
容積率：制限493.18％＞実効91.77％
構造と規模：S造　地上２階建て
敷地面積：834.49㎡　建築面積：463.15㎡
床面積：１階470.73㎡　２階295.09㎡（うち厨房99.85㎡）　合計765.82㎡
工期：1993年２月10日～４月26日
総工費：３億円
解体撤去費100万円　建築躯体工事費１億4830万円　外構工事費300万円　サイン3300万円　内装造作費2800万円　空調設備費1600万円　厨房設備費1100万円　給排水衛生設備費1200万円　電気設備費3250万円　照明器具費570万円　家具・什器費750万円　音響設備費200万円
●営業内容
〈ナイキショップ＆３オン３コート〉
開店：1993年４月27日
営業時間：午前11時～午後８時
電話：（03）3423-6008　定休日：なし
経営者：㈱ナイキジャパン
従業員：３人　客単価：１万円
主な取り扱い商品と単価：靴１万2000～２万1000　バスケットコート使用料（１時間）500（高校生以下は300）
〈「ホットドッグカフェ」＆「ザ・プレイヤーズ」〉
開店：1993年４月27日　定休日：なし
営業時間：午前11時～午後８時（２階は午後11時まで）
電話：１階（03）35410-5043　２階35410-5044
経営者：㈱ワコールアートセンター
従業員：１階／９人　２階／14人
客席数：１階／80席　２階／86席
客単価：１階／800円　２階／3000円
客回転数：１階／４～６回　２階／３～４回
主なメニューと単価：１階／ホットドック330　２階／ザ・プレイヤーズスペシャルリブ2450　アジックスストロベリージュース700
●主な仕上げ材料
屋根：長尺カラー折板t0.6断熱仕様（ヨドルーフ）
外壁：ノンアスベストフレキシブルボードt６横貼り　長尺カラー鉄板t0.4貼りロックウール吹き付け
外部床：マットスラブコンクリート下地防浸塗装　樹脂系塗り床材（ニューカラートップP／ABC商会）
サイン：スチールフラットバー６×50組みのうえネコキャンバスシート張り　スチールメラミン焼き付け塗装　粘着シート貼り（ファラオン・ホワイトベース／シーエスエイ）
床：マットスラブコンクリート下地黒モルタル金ゴテ押さえt30　サクラ材フローリングt15　CL　コンクリート下地エポキシ樹脂系塗り床材塗り分け（ケミクリート／ABC商会）
壁：軽鉄組みPBt12下地寒冷紗パテシゴキVP　コンクリート打ち放し　スクリーン／スチール丸パイプφ60枠組みネコキャンバスシート張り　ファラオン・ホワイトベース貼り
天井：デッキプレート葺きVP
家具：「アリーフープ」／アメリカナイキショップ仕様　「ホットドッグコート」／アンビエンテインターナショナル　「ザ・プレイヤース」／椅子＆テーブル・合羽橋洋家具
什器：「アリーフープ」／ナイキ仕様ハムロックシステム　シミュレーションジム／高画質スクリーン＆体感システム（DMSシートスクリーンシステム／ショースキャン）
●撮影：野口　毅（'93年８月号）

UCCカフェプラザ 新宿店・データ（P152）

工事種別：ファサードと内装　全面改装
床面積：102㎡（うち厨房18㎡）
工期：1990年５月21日～６月22日
●営業内容
開店：1990年６月23日
営業時間：午前８時～午後９時
定休日：なし　電話：（03）3352-1638
経営者：上島珈琲㈱
従業員：サービス１人　厨房３人　パート・アルバイト常時４人　合計８人
客席数：56席
客単価：560円　客回転数：５回
主なメニューと単価：コーヒー500　ケーキ各種500　ケーキセット800　モーニングセット550～700　ビール550　コーヒーカクテル各種680～750
●主な仕上げ材料
床：タイル貼り150角（名古屋モザイク工業）　ナラ材フローリング着色ウレタン仕上げ
壁：白セメント金ゴテ仕上げレンガチップ埋め込み　30×30L形アングルメラミン焼き付け塗装　スチールスクリーンt５ウレタン系塗料（ボンスエード／武蔵塗装）　アクリルスクリーンカラーフィルム貼り
天井：既存の上EP　一部間接照明器具内蔵
照明器具：カウンター上部ペンダント／ガラスカラーフィルム貼りおよびパンチングメタル壁面ブラケット／30×30L形アングル
●撮影：平井広行（'90年11月号）

カフェ・ド・マルティニーク・データ（P156）

工事種別：一戸建て　新築
用途地域地区：商業地域
建ぺい率：制限100％＞実効75.2％
容積率：制限800％＞実効85.0％
構造と規模：S造（簡易耐火構造）　地上２階建て
敷地面積：117.569㎡　建築面積：88.444㎡
床面積：１階79.868㎡　２階20.114㎡　合計99.982㎡（うち厨房13.250㎡）
工期：1989年12月１日～1990年３月20日
総工費：3000万円
●営業内容
開店：1990年３月24日
営業時間：平日／午前11時～午後11時　日曜・祭日／午前11時30分～午後７時30分
定休日：なし　電話：（03）3207-9555
経営者：深谷稔彦
従業員：サービス１人　厨房２人　パート・アルバイト常時２人　合計５人
客席数：64席（テラス席を含む）
客単価：900円　客回転数：2.5回
主なメニューと単価：ランチセット1000・1300　ナスのグラタン500　スパゲッティ900～1300　ケーキ400～450　コーヒー500　ビール600～700
●主な仕上げ材料
屋根：木毛板下地亜鉛引き鉄板貼り
外壁：ALC板アクリルリシン吹き付け　開口部／スチールフレーム・アルミサッシュ網入りガラスt6.8
外部床：テラス／土間コンクリート下地足場板（杉）貼りt30
サイン：テント　フラッグ
床：客室／土間コンクリート下地足場（杉）貼りt30　厨房／土間コンクリート下地モルタル金ゴテ仕上げ
壁：客席／ALC板下地鏡貼り　一部布ドレープ吊り　風除室・厨房外壁・トイレ／白モルタル金ゴテ仕上げ　柱・梁／鉄骨（古材）サビ出し仕上げ
天井：木毛板木綿布吊り込み（一部可動式）　天窓／スチールフレーム網入り型板ガラスt6.8
照明器具：スポットライト／ハロゲン球＋ビーム球（遠藤照明）
家具：テーブル／米松材ムクOSCL　カウンター／ブビンガ材CL
●撮影：飯嶋祐司（'90年11月号）

カフェ ミラノ・データ（P158）

工事種別：一戸建て　新築
用途地域地区：商業地域
建ぺい率：制限80％＞実効23.4％
容積率：制限500％＞実効23.4％
構造と規模：S造平屋建て
敷地面積：417.3㎡　建築面積：365.0㎡
床面積：365.0㎡（うち厨房54.0㎡）
工期：1990年３月１日～４月11日
総工費：6000万円
●営業内容
営業期間：1990年４月13日～６月30日
営業時間：午前11時～午後９時
定休日：なし
経営者：とらばーゆ／㈱リクルート
運営：カフェ／キム＆ケイズ
従業員：インフォメーションカウンター６人　カフェ５人　合計11人
客席数：92席　客単価：700円
主なメニューと単価：サンドイッチ250～350　ポテトグラタン400　ランチセット700～850　エスプレッソ200　ビール400　ワイン400
●主な仕上げ材料
屋根：耐火ボード下地カラー鉄板葺き
外壁：フレキシブルボード二重貼りAEPエージング仕上げ　壁画／アクリル塗料（リキテックス／バニーコーポレーション）
外部床：耐水合板二重貼り下地長尺塩ビシート貼り
サイン：パーティクルボード（ライオンボード／東洋ベニヤ工業）アクリル塗装
床：耐水合板二重貼り下地強化リノリウム床材（アーマタイル／L.S.I）
壁：軽鉄組みPBt12下地AEPエージング仕上げ
天井：軽鉄組みPBt９下地AEPエージング仕上げ　天井画／アクリル塗料（リキテックス／バニーコーポレーション）
●撮影：鈴木　光（'90年10月号）

イースト ギャラリー・データ（P161）

工事種別：内装のみ　部分改装
床面積：262.44㎡（うち厨房21.6㎡）
工期：1991年12月１日～1992年１月12日
●営業内容
開店：1992年１月13日
営業時間：午前11時～午後10時
定休日：なし　経営者：E.B.C.inc.
従業員：サービス２人　厨房３人　パート・アルバイト常時３人　合計８人
客席数：40席　客単価：1200円
主なメニューと単価：トーフフリターダ700　ベジタブルパイ700　ケーキセット700　ランチ（サンドイッチ　スープ　コーヒー）1000　コーヒー400　紅茶400　ペリエ500　スパニッシュシャンパン（グラス）700　ビール（ハイネケン）700　グラスワイン600
●主な仕上げ材料
床：コンクリート平板300×600t60敷き込み　一部玉砂利敷き詰め
壁：既存RC打ち放し　一部木軸組みの上シナ合板貼りSOP
天井：既存RC打ち放し　一部木軸組みの上に化粧割り竹目透かし貼り
照明器具：マックスレイ
カウンター：側板／シナ合板貼りSOP　甲板／鉄板t６の上フロストガラスt12
什器：PC板製プランターボックスφ1200　H900
●撮影：野口　毅（'92年９月号）

作品データ

データ内容は雑誌掲載時のものです

ボアン デュ ジュール・データ(P164)

工事種別：内装のみ　新築
床面積：75.0㎡(うち厨房7.5㎡)
工期：1992年9月1日～10月15日
総工費：2970万円
内装造作費1580万円　厨房設備費150万円
給排水衛生設備費15万円　電気設備費220万円
照明器具費155万円　家具・什器費850万円
●営業内容
開店：1992年11月4日
営業時間：午前10時～午後7時
定休日：日曜・祭日　電話：(03)3485-8075
経営者：㈱ザ・サン田中
従業員：2人　パート・アルバイト1人　合計3人
客席数：25席　客単価(カフェ)：500円
主なメニューと単価：コーヒー・紅茶・ジュース500
主な取り扱い商品と単価：アクセサリー3000～9000　ハンドバッグ9000～2万　時計9000～1万4000
●主な仕上げ材料
床：石灰岩貼り(ストローブホーン／アドヴァン)
壁：PBt12下地AEP海綿特殊塗装(ぬり貫)　一部染色人工突き板(ダンウッドパール／日東紡績)
天井：PBt12下地AEP海綿特殊塗装(ぬり貫)
家具：大彌リビング　什器：ダンウッドパール
●撮影：鈴木　光('93年4月号)

ア ポイント・データ(P167)

工事種別：ファサードと内装　全面改装
床面積：1階391.38㎡(うち厨房78.95㎡)　2階124.03㎡　合計515.41㎡
工期：1990年9月1日～1991年2月14日
総工費：3億2300万円
●営業内容
開店：1991年2月14日
営業時間：午前8時～午後10時
定休日：日曜・祭日　電話：(03)3216-4808
経営者：㈱パッセンジャーズ・サービス
従業員：サービス4人　厨房7人　パート・アルバイト常時20人　合計31人
客席数：188席
客単価：1600円　客回転数：5回
主なメニューと単価：デニッシュ・ペストリー150～　オーダーサンド450　サラダ各種500　オードブル各種500　ポテトグラタン450　輸入缶ビール各種550
●主な仕上げ材料
外壁：鉄骨組み大理石貼り本磨き(ビアンコカララ)　スチール角パイプおよびスチールプレートt1.6曲げ加工OP塗装三分ツヤ
床：1階／モルタル下地テラゾ貼り(ナチュラーレマーブル／フッコー)　2階／モルタル下地フローリング乱尺貼りW90
幅木：合板t9染色ウレタン塗装半ツヤ
壁：PBt12VP塗装半ツヤ　腰壁／カバ単板練り付けケイカル板t6染色CL半ツヤ
天井：軽鉄組みPBt12二重貼りVP塗装半ツヤ
照明器具：マックスレイ
対面ショーケース：マイヤービストー社(ドイツ)
●撮影：ナカサ&パートナーズ('91年11月号)

ラ フィエスタ・データ(P170)

工事種別：内装のみ　新築
床面積：521.15㎡
工期：1992年8月3日～11月30日
●営業内容
開店：1992年12月6日
営業時間：午前6時30分～午後10時
定休日：なし　電話：(0476)34-6190
経営者：㈱ティエフケー
従業員：20人　客席数：188席
客単価：880円　客回転数：10.8回
主なメニューと単価：英国風ビーフカレー980　屋台風汁麺780　おろし牛丼980　コーヒー350　生ビール500
●主な仕上げ材料
床：レッドシダーフローリング　白大理石貼りt15
壁：PBt15下地塩ビ化粧シート貼り(ベルビアン／シーアイ化成)
天井：ケイカル板t6下地AP
ブース：集成材　松柾練り付け
●撮影：香川康之('93年4月号)

アリスのテーブル・データ(P173)

工事種別：一戸建て　新築
用途地域地区：指定なし(国立公園内)
構造と規模：S造　平屋建て
建築面積：560.95㎡
床面積：560.95㎡(うち厨房120.00㎡)
工期：1991年12月10日～1992年7月20日(遊園地全体)
●営業内容
開店：1992年7月20日
営業時間：午前10時～午後6時(冬季は5時，夏休みおよびゴールデンウイークは午後9時まで)
定休日：なし　電話：(0977)22-1165(代表)
経営者：㈱西日本後楽園
従業員：サービス3人　厨房2人　パート・アルバイト常時4人　合計9人
客席数：店内130席　テラス100席
客単価：700円　客回転数：6回
主なメニューと単価：インディアンカレー500　テリヤキバーガー330　チキン&ポテト400　コーラ・オレンジジュースM180　L220　コーヒー200
●主な仕上げ材料
屋根：耐火野地板t18+アスファルトルーフィング22kg下地化粧繊維セメント板(カラーベストコロニアル／クボタ)
外壁：アスファルトフェルト22kg+ケイカル板t10下地アクリルリシン吹き付け　化粧木片セメント板貼り(センチュリーボードよこばり木目／三井木材工業)　アクリルエマルション系塗装　開口部／スチールサッシSOP　透明ガラスt8
外部床：コンクリート下地アクリルウレタン樹脂塗装(ユタック-R／日本特殊塗料)
サイン：木下地アクリル板文字貼り
床：弾性モルタル下地アクリルウレタン樹脂塗装2色模様塗り(ユタックS／日本特殊塗料)
幅木：白ラワン材OSCL　H100
壁：磁器タイルパターン貼り150角(イナックス)
天井：ケイカル板t6下地塩化ビニルエナメル塗装(3色)
家具：小椅子(フォルコラ／アカデミア)　ベンチ(ダイコー)
カウンター：腰／木軸組みシナ合板下地塩ビシート貼り(ダイノックシート／住友スリーエム)　甲板／ステンレスHL
●撮影：ナカサ&パートナーズ('93年7月号)

みずは北川 祇園店・データ(P176)

工事種別：内装のみ　全面改装
床面積：地下1階84㎡　1階86㎡　中2階29㎡　合計199㎡(うち厨房29㎡)
工期：1991年10月1日～10月30日
総工費：7211万円
建築軀体工事費432万円　内装造作費4200万円　空調設備費640万円　厨房設備費900万円　給排水衛生設備費161万円　電気設備費333万円　照明器具費105万円　家具・什器費440万円
●営業内容
開店：1991年11月1日
営業時間：正午～午後9時
定休日：なし　電話：(075)531-4146
経営者：㈱光明舎　北川　明
従業員：サービス4人　厨房3人　パート・アルバイト常時6人　合計13人
客席数：70席
客単価：1500円　客回転数：4回
主なメニューと単価：販売／生麩まんじゅう5個1100　10個2200　喫茶／生麩まんじゅう+抹茶1000　上生菓子+煎茶1000　団子+ほうじ茶1000　チーズケーキ+コーヒー1000
●主な仕上げ材料
床：黒御影石ジェットバーナー仕上げ　クラッシュタイル貼り(イナックス)
壁：軽鉄組みPBt12下地スエード調塗材(ネオドット／アサヒペン)　漆喰壁状仕上げ塗材(ナプコホワイト／関西ペイント)　スクリーン／スチールプレートメラミン焼き付け塗装　スチールプレートフラッシュ色ラッカー吹き付け塗装
天井：軽鉄組みPBt12下地ナプコホワイト
テーブル：天板／米ヒノキ材　脚／ステンレススチール
販売カウンター：黒御影石水磨き　クリアガラスt12
サービスカウンター：天板／稲田石t20　腰／クラッシュタイル
●撮影：藤原　弘(＊は川元　斉)('92年4月号)

フロマージュウ・データ(P178)

工事種別：内装のみ　新築
床面積：95.75㎡(うち厨房35.31㎡)
工期：1990年8月1日～9月20日
総工費：1500万円
●営業内容
開店：1990年9月23日
営業時間：午前9時～午後9時
定休日：木曜日　電話：(075)921-5565
経営者：㈱フロマージュウ　片岡広司
従業員：サービス2人　厨房4人　合計6人
客席数：8席
客単価：1600円　客回転数：3回
主なメニューと単価：チーズケーキ280　ティラミス400　抹茶セット680　珈琲セット650
●主な仕上げ材料
床：モルタル金ゴテ押さえの上に琉球畳，白川砂，グレーチング敷き　一部シナ合板ウレタン塗装
壁：軽鉄組みコンパネt12下地アルミ亜鉛合金メッキ鋼板(ガルバリウム鋼板／大同鋼板)　平板ビス止め貼り　腰壁／ガルバリウム鋼板小波板ビス止め貼り　金・銀紙千鳥貼り屏風
天井：軽鉄組みコンパネt12下地ガルバリウム鋼板平板ビス止め貼り
カウンターテーブル：シナ合板t40ウレタン塗装
●撮影：藤原　弘('91年5月号)